Forgery of the
Old Testament

AND OTHER ESSAYS

THE

Forgery of the
Old Testament

AND OTHER ESSAYS

Joseph
McCabe

 Prometheus Books

59 John Glenn Drive
Buffalo, NewYork 14228-2197

Published 1993 by Prometheus Books
59 John Glenn Drive, Buffalo, New York 14228-2197,
716-837-2475. FAX: 716-835-6901.

Library of Congress Cataloging-in-Publication Data

McCabe, Joseph, 1867–1955.
    The forgery of the Old Testament, and other essays / Joseph
McCabe.
        p.   cm. — (The Freethought library)
    Originally published separately by Haldeman-Julius Co., Girard,
Kan. 1926–27 and issued as no. 1248, 1059, and 1066 of the series:
Little blue book.
    Contents: The forgery of the Old Testament — The myth of
immortality — Lies of religious literature.
    ISBN 0-87975-850-3 (paper)
    1. Bible. O.T.—Controverail literature. 2. Immortality.
3. Christianity—Controversial literature. I. McCabe, Joseph, 1867–
1955. Myth of immortality. 1993. II. McCabe, Joseph, 1867–1955.
Lies of religious literature. 1993. III. Title. IV. Series.
BS1179.M335   1993
230—dc20   93-27365
                                                                        CIP

Printed in the United States of America on acid-free paper.

THE FREETHOUGHT LIBRARY

Featuring Selections from the Haldeman-Julius Collection

Over a period of thirty years, publisher E. Haldeman-Julius made available to millions of readers inexpensive paperback editions of classics of literature and freethought. Prometheus is proud to be reissuing selected numbers of the renowned Blue Books, *which provided a broad forum for the discussion of rationalist issues.*

Additional Titles in
The Freethought Library

Debates on the Meaning of Life, Evolution, and Spiritualism
Frank Harris, Percy Ward, George McCready Price,
Joseph McCabe, and Sir Arthur Conan Doyle

The Myth of the Resurrection and Other Essays
Joseph McCabe

The Necessity of Atheism and Other Essays
Percy Bysshe Shelley

Reason, Tolerance, and Christianity
The Ingersoll Debates
Robert G. Ingersoll

JOSEPH MARTIN MCCABE was born on November 11, 1867, of a Catholic working class family in Macclesfield, England. At the age of sixteen, Joseph entered the Franciscan seminary; upon his ordination at twenty-three, Joseph—now Father Anthony—was appointed to teach philosophy. However, the young priest began increasingly to doubt the truth of the Catholic religion. Finally, after weighing the evidence for and against belief in God and immortality and finding his faith "bankrupt," McCabe promptly abandoned both the priesthood and Catholicism.

Through the offices of his friend Sir Leslie Stephen, McCabe began a prodigious writing career, beginning with his autobiographical *Twelve Years in a Monastery* (1897). Following the success of this work, McCabe turned to biographies and translations. His translation in 1902 of Ernst Haeckel's *The Riddle of the Universe* spread McCabe's reputation throughout the English-speaking world.

Influenced by Haeckel's defense of organic evolution and its ramifications for science, philosophy, and theology, McCabe applied this same evolutionary view to the study of history: History, he argued, was to be regarded not merely as a record of events but as a scientific understanding of the development of human culture and social institutions. Human history, therefore, in line with the deterministic materialism of Karl Marx, was moving away from religion and oppressive monarchies and toward science and social equality, which would culminate in an enlightened new age. The threat to human progress, however, lay in the Church and its alliance with the bourgeoisie. McCabe saw this as a lethal union responsible for fascism in Europe and an assault upon communism and socialism, which McCabe regarded as harbingers of his new world order.

In the earlier part of this century McCabe was on friendly terms with the leading skeptics in English intellectual and political life; he produced many of his books in connection with the British Rationalist Association. However, McCabe's aggressive

7

candor and fractiousness led to his increasing isolation, the breakup of his marriage in 1925, and his expulsion from the British Rationalist Association in 1928. From the late 1920s until his death, McCabe wrote almost exclusively for E. Haldeman-Julius, who—touting McCabe as "the world's greatest scholar"—published his work at least 300 Little Blue Books and 200 larger volumes, which caustically inveighed against the evils and follies of organized religion.

Despite misfortunes in his personal life, McCabe remained an optimist and an unflinching foe of "bishops, preachers, exploiters of the poor, millionaires, parasites, dictators, and liars and crooks generally." Joseph McCabe died, in his eighty-eighth year, on January 10, 1955.

McCabe's important books include: *A Biographical Dictionary of Modern Rationalists, The Life and Letters of George Jacob Holyoake, The Decay of the Church of Rome, The Sources of the Mortality of the Gospels,* and *A Rationalist Encyclopedia.*

Contents

The Forgery of the
Old Testament

1

The Romance of the Old Testament

In the years 597 and 596 before the Christian Era pathetic caravans set out from Jerusalem and the hills of Judea for the distant civilization of Babylonia. Three thousand three and twenty men of the Jewish race were being deported. It is a remarkably precise figure for a prophet to give us, so we will believe him. When we count the wives and children, which he disdains to do, we gather that more than ten thousand of the children of Abraham were setting out on one of those journeys for which their race would later be famous.

A pathetic sight, certainly: if common enough in those days. We picture the dejected Jews, their dark eyes veiled in sorrow or kindling with momentary anger, and the escorts of thick-bearded, swarthy, large-bodied Babylonian soldiers. Over the fords of the Jordan, across the sultry and choking desert, they drag their limbs day after day and week after week, probably for six or seven weeks. The vultures look on from the hills. The jackals peep at them from afar. They are rebels against Babylonian majesty, entitled to no consideration, lucky to retain their lives.

Long before that the Assyrians had shattered the northern half of their race, the kingdom of Israel, and herded thousands of them to Mesopotamia. Now the children of Judah followed,

13

wondering why Jahveh was so silent. And those who remained at home forgot the terrible lesson and, eleven years later, again rebelled; and five years later again rebelled. "Root them out of their rocky ledges," said the great king Nebuchadnezzar. And, in all, about twenty thousand of them wet the desert route with their tears; and the pride of Judaism, the great temple, the splendid palace, the public buildings, were razed.

By the rivers of Babylon they sat and wept—some of them. It was a much fairer land, this broad plain between the two great rivers: this "Eden"—which is simply the Babylonian name for plain, just as "Eben" (or *Ebene*) is the word in German today. What groves of palms and teeming orchards! What wonderful harvests three times a year! And many would settle in, or eventually reach, Babylon, the greatest city of the world. How mean the narrow, tortuous, dirty streets of Jerusalem would seem in comparison with these broad quays and roads and squares, the walls shining in the sun with their beautiful glazed-brick fronts, the palaces and their "hanging gardens" lining the routes, the vast temples towering four hundred feet above the roofs!

The Babylonian would not trouble about them. These "frontier wars" were always bringing thousands of semicivilized people into exile in Babylonia. Why couldn't the weird-looking fanatics pay their tribute quietly and stop at home? And some of them were pretty sharp, and began to compete in the civil service and at the court.

Probably a thoughtful man here and there talked to his neighbor about them, or, when they learned the language, dropped into conversation with them. What would he make of the Jews in the middle of the sixth century B.C.?

A pastoral, rather primitive people, he would say, probably numbering a hundred thousand or so, scattered over a modest and very stony area which they called their kingdom. Nominally they had one god, but they were very partial to other people's gods. Code of morals—"ten commandments," they call them— very rough and scanty. Literature a few old poems, some amusing chronicles, certain curious effusions which they call prophecies, and a very drastic priest-book which they call their Law.

Mainly farmers, with a few large villages and a town of about twenty thousand people—since practically all Jerusalem must have been deported—containing a temple and a palace which they thought very grand until they came to Babylon.

Babylon fell to the Persians in 539; and there were Zionists who urged King Cyrus, whom they regarded as an ancient President Wilson, a liberator of subject peoples, to let them return. Yes, if you like, he said; for his new empire was restless, and it was well to have friends in the far west. How many went we do not know; but even less than those who left New York and Chicago for liberated Palestine in 1920. And northerners and southerners entered into a petty civil war, so that nothing could be done. Jerusalem remained almost as gaunt as Ypres. The more enterprising emigrated to Egypt or Persia, and (as inscriptions tell) made wealth and names. You could have bought Judea with a small fortune. A learned Greek, Herodotus, visited the country at the time, gathering material for the first history of the human race. He does not mention the Jews.

Yet when Egyptian and Babylonian, Persian and Greek, went down into their tombs, the Jews began to conquer the world. Two thousand five hundred years after the great King Nebuchadnezzar lay on his ivory and gold couch, and cursed these savages of the Syrian hills, the fragments of his mighty empire and its culture would be patiently dug out of the dust, while the sacred book of the Jews would be kissed reverently all over the world, in the law-courts of prouder cities than Persian or Babylonian ever saw. Who, do you ask, was Marduk? Who was Ahura Mazda? Who was Horus? Thin shades of the mightiest gods of long ago. And Jahveh today rules forty civilizations so rich that one man in them could have bought up Egypt and Baylonia: so learned that a child of twelve knows more than all the sages of Chaldea: so modern that they . . . enthrone the sacred book of the Jews in their hearts and homes, their schools and courts, their camps and temples.

That is the real romance of the Jew, his sacred book. Oh, it is not unique. Do not begin to look for supernatural rea-

sons. The Koran has even more worshipers, to count only genuine worshipers, and it had no higher source. Hindu and Bud-
dhist books have quite as many.

Yet it is one of the great romances of religious evolution,
and we have to understand it. As usual, let us face it candidly.
The Bible is not retained in modern civilization because it is
"great literature." That is no reason for believing it, and let-
ting it rule civilization. It is not retained because it is "a unique
account of the development of a people and its religion." It
is, on the contrary, almost a unique falsification of the history
of a people and its religion. The Old Testament, together with
the New Testament, rules us—is read with honor in the very
modern schools of America, is handled reverently in court, closes
theaters on a Sunday in England, and so on—solely because
hundreds of millions of people, before whom politicians trem-
ble and editors dissemble, believe that it is "the Word of God."

It is part of the Bible. The Jews, some time before the
Babylonian Captivity, treasured only "the Law": a very small
book, probably, but we are not quite sure what it was. With
this they later began to treasure "the Prophets." In the end they
had quite a number of sacred and semi-sacred books. The Greek
word for "books" is "biblia," so, as it was through the Greek
Christian world that these books came to dominate civilization,
they are called, collectively, the *biblia* or bible. Anybody who
questioned anything in them was burned.

After the tyranny of Rome had been shattered by the
Reformers, some liberty to think and speak was won. The Reformers really transferred the tyranny to the book, but the modern era had opened, and scholars began to talk about the book:
not to think and reason about it—there is plenty of evidence
that they had done that since the twelfth century, but it was
indiscreet to say what they thought. Now there arose a school
of Deists who, while they believed in God, drastically examined
and rejected the Bible!

About the end of the eighteenth century really learned men,
mostly Protestant divines, began this work in earnest. The Deists
had been superficial. The "Higher Critics" went on the principles

of modern science and modern history. For more than a hundred years now they have been examining the Old Testament; and, considering the circumstances—they are, and have always been, practically all sincere and learned clergymen—they have come to a remarkable amount of agreement. The development of science, meantime, has helped. The development of archeology and history has helped even more.

I am not going here simply to give you a summary of what are called "the results of the Higher Criticism." Very largely, we are going to study the Old Testament for ourselves. But we use their work, insofar as you can verify it with your own eyes by consulting our Bible. We may differ from them often, and we will try to be broadminded and reasonable. But to begin with I am going to express the general result in language of my own which, they will agree with you, is shocking. The end of the great romance is the discovery that the Old Testament is a forgery.

2

How We Detect the Forgery

The Word of God a forgery! I can understand the bewilderment of a religious reader, but let him consider coolly what the statement means. It does not mean that God forged a book. It means that men forged a book in his name. That can be examined dispassionately by anybody.

But, you say, they were religious men, and the charge is an insult. My dear friend, Protestant divines and preachers *unanimously* accuse, not merely religious men, but ministers of the Christian Gospel of hundreds of forgeries.

You never heard of it? Why, they hold—and quite rightly—that almost all the stories of saints and martyrs which are treasured in the Roman Church are forgeries; and there are Roman Catholic scholars who agree with them. They hold—all the non-Roman historians in the world hold—that the documents on which the power of Rome is essentially based are sheer forgeries. They hold that from the sixth to the twelfth century Roman priests poured upon Europe a flood of forgeries, very much to their own profit.

The simple question here is whether ancient Jewish priests had done the same thing a thousand years before. But that is different, you say. These supposed forgeries are not lives of saints and decrees of councils, but the Word of God.

That is precisely the issue. Who says so? Just think a little. The belief that the Old Testament is the Word of God is your fundamental belief: it is the essence of fundamentalism. Did you ever reflect on your grounds for that belief? It is a thousand to one that you have not. You resist evolution and science—you scoff at the united authority of all the experts in the world—because they contradict the Word of God. And you never thought of asking yourself *how you know* that it is. The claim of a book to be by a certain author is no evidence at all. You require external proof. Did Bryan or Riley ever give you that? But Christ. . . . Patience. You cannot quote the authority of Christ until we have examined the New Testament.

Well, then, what *is* a forgery? It is a deliberate falsification or fabrication of documents or of the signature to them. A letter, a poem (like "Ossian's" poems), an historical work (like some "found" recently in Italy), a will, a bank note, a postage stamp even, may be forged.

Now the far greater part of the more learned clerical authorities on the Bible say that many books of the Old Testament pretend to be written by men who did not write them; that many books were deliberately written as history when the writers knew that they were not history; and that the Old Testament as a whole, as we have it, is a deliberate attempt to convey an historical belief which the writers knew to be false.

But these learned authorities do not like the word forgery. It is crude. Let me give you a few illustrations, from easily accessible and weighty works, of what they do say. It will at least show you the elegance, the subtlety, the resources of diplomatic language.

The article "Israel" in the *Encyclopaedia Biblica,* a Christian work, is written by Professor Guthe, a learned theologian of Leipsic University. He says that the writers of the Old Testament have a "mode of regarding the facts" in which we can see "the workings of a primitive nature." He says that the poor historian of the Jews had a hard job "to remove the materials of his story out of the *false light* in which he finds them." He must "constantly bear in mind the pecularities of the narrative"; and he frankly tells you that these are "their *legendary character,* their *conformity to a scheme,* and their *didactic purpose.*" Does it not sound very much like an extremely polite description of what plain men call a forgery?

The article "David" is by another famous theologian, Professor Marti. He says that "keen criticism is necessary to arrive at the kernel of fact" in the familiar story of David; and that some very learned theologians "deny that there is such a kernel of fact." Most theologians, however, he says, believe that "the *imaginative element* in the story of David is but the vesture which half conceals, half discloses, certain facts treasured in popular tradition." Nice language, isn't it?

Dr. Cheyne, recently a very high dignitary of the Church of England, writes on "Abraham." When he has done with the patriarch, we have only a tissue of "*legends* purified both by abridgment *and expression.*" After all, that is only what the Koran did with Mohammed.

Professor Moore, of Andover Theological Seminary, writes the article in "Historical Literature." He thinks that the early historical writers of the Old Testament—not in the time of Moses, but centuries later; and not as we have their works now—were honest collectors of stories, but that later books were put together by the "mere literary process of conflation and contamination." Hard words. The scribes, he says, "combined different copies according to their own judgment *and interests.*" This gives us "a different religious point of view—in plain English, a view of the facts which is not true—but the scribes merely acted "in a prophetic spirit." In the end (as we shall see) another set of writers recast the whole of these honest legends and dishonest "contaminations," and added a vast amount of new matter (expressly ascribing it to Moses) for which, Professor Moore says, they probably had no sources—except their imagination and "interests." The result is our Old Testament.

But the *Encyclopaedia Biblica* is full of this from cover to cover of its four large volumes. Let us try the *Encyclopaedia Britannica.* Alas, it is just as bad. Professor Cook, of Cambridge University, says (article "Jews"): "Written by Oriental people, clothed in an Oriental dress, the Old Testament does not contain *objective* records," but "*subjective* history for specific purposes." One would like to hear a perjured witness in court defend himself on the ground that his statements were sound subjective history for a specific purpose. "Scholars are now almost unanimously agreed" on these manipulations, he says. But they have really rendered you a service. The Higher Criticism has "brought into relief the central truths which really are vital." What truths, you ask? Why, that the Old Testament gradually evolved from the tenth to the second century, and in its present form is mainly a fifth-century compilation so distorting the facts that it has taken scholars a hundred and fifty years to get them straight.

Enough of these Higher Critics, you say: you know that I could quote a hundred of them. Well, let us take a learned Protestant divine, the Reverend Professor Sayce, of Oxford University, who is a vigorous opponent of Higher Critics. His chief work, *The Higher Criticism and the Verdict of the Monuments,* published by the Society for the Promotion of Christian Knowledge, is the standard criticism of the Higher Criticism. Let us hear him, by all means; and I am going to take first a part of his work which will at the same time enable you to judge at once whether there are forgeries in the Old Testament and show you how we detect them.

You know well the book of *Daniel.* Some scenes of that vivid narrative, such as the famous feast of "Belshazzar the King" and the writing on the wall, have passed into the art and letters of the world. It expressly says throughout that it was written by Daniel himself. "I Daniel" occurs in every chapter.

Some time ago we recovered tablets of the great Persian king Cyrus, and Professor Sayce gives us a translation of them; and he compares them, as you may, with the words of *Daniel*: "In that night was Belshazzar the king of the Chaldeans slain, and Darius the Median took the kingdom." The tablets of Cyrus describe the taking of Babylon, and are beyond the slightest suspicion. The Persians had adopted the Babylonian custom of writing on clay, then baking the brick or tablet, and such documents last forever. And these and other authentic and contemporary documents of the age which "Daniel" describes show:

1. That Belshazzar was not king of Babylon.

2. That the name of the last king was Nabonidos.

3. That the city was taken peacefully, by guile, not by bloodshed.

4. That it was Cyrus, not Darius the Median, who took it.

5. That Darius, who is said (xi, 1) by Daniel to have been the son of "Ahasuerus" (Xerxes), was really his father.

6. That all the Babylonian names in Daniel are absurdly misspelled and quite strange to the writer.

7. That the writer describes the Chaldeans in a way that no writer could have done before the time of Alexander the Great.

You can read the rest of the critic of the Higher Critics. It is now beyond question that the man who wrote *Daniel,* and pretended to be alive in 539 B.C. (when Babylon fell), did not live until three or four centuries later. The book is a tissue of errors, as we find by authentic documents and by reading the real Babylonian names on the tablets.

Now why did the writer do it, and what was his object? Quite clearly he wanted to convince the Jews that Jahveh would miraculously protect any Jews who refused to obey a sacrilegious king. And this gives us the clue to the date. It was in the second century B.C., when the Greek king Antiochus Epiphanes tried to compel the Jews to break their law. A pious Jew, probably a priest, then wrote this book: very clumsily, as in the course of three centuries the facts and names had been forgotten. Now we have recovered the real contemporary documents, and there is no room for dispute.

Well, is that a forgery? Sayce concludes leniently that it is "not historical in the modern sense of the word history"! Others blandly tell us that it was "a work of edification," one of the "hagiographa" (which means "*holy* writings"). You are asked to remember "the nature of the Oriental mind," which is so very different from the American. These superficial writers who talk of forgery, you are told, do not know the Oriental mind.

I know it well, and I know this: If you were to tell an Oriental Mohammedan that the wonderful things said about the Prophet in the Koran were "subjective history with a specific purpose," he would, when he learned precisely what you meant, knock you down. The Oriental loves stories, but he has as keen a sense as any of the difference between stories and sacred history. *Daniel* pretended to be history. Otherwise it would have had no effect. It is a forgery.

And Professor Sayce goes on to show that *Ezra, Tobit* and *Judith*—the latter are in the Catholic Bible—are on the same level. "The decipherment of the cuneiform inscriptions," he says, "has finally destroyed all claim on the part of the Books of *Tobit* and *Judith* to be considered as history" (p. 552). It does not much matter that they are not in the Protestant canon. They are examples of ancient Jewish forgeries. Professor Sayce shows the same for familiar Bible stories like those of Susanna and Bel and the Dragon. In fact, this remarkable book, which sets out to destroy the Higher Critics, begins with decisive proof that *Genesis* is a compilation of Babylonian legends (ascribed to Moses) and ends with the exposures I have given!

You see now how we detect forgeries. There are two chief ways: the style of the documents and the testimony of other and undisputed documents. The second method I have illustrated; and, now that we have recovered such a mass of ancient literature, it covers a great deal of the Old Testament.

The first method, to judge a literary writing by its literary style, has been much ridiculed by pious people; and the ridicule is ridiculous. On the orthodox theory the Old Testament was written at different periods during more than a thousand years. Now there is not a language known that does not change so much in the course of centuries that even a child can see the difference at a glance. The inexpert reader will find it almost impossible to read the earliest English literature. Even as late as the eighteenth century, English was written quite differently from the way in which we write it today. Literary experts can tell at once whether a French, Italian, German, or English book was written in the thirteenth (like Dante's Italian), sixteenth, or nineteenth century.

So we can with Hebrew, because even on the most advanced theory the writing of the Old Testament covers seven hundred years. And this is the simple method of the higher Critics, which preachers who do not know a word of Hebrew— and could not even themselves read the English of Chaucer— ridicule. This method confidently shows us fragments of different ages in the Old Testament put together at a far later date. Further, we find inconsistencies, contradictions, and duplications which cannot otherwise be explained. Now, in addition, we have a very great deal of history and archeology by which we can check the Old Testament. These collective tests make up the Higher Criticism, a scientific study, and we will see what the result is. But it will be convenient first to see a little of the history of the Jews insofar as it bears upon the writing of the Old Testament.

3

The Priestly Forgers

What I mean when I say that the Old Testament was "forged" will now be fairly clear. In the first place, whole books, like *Daniel,* are what we call in modern English forgeries; and, if the Jews of 2,200 or even 2,500 years ago had known the real origin of them, they would have called them forgeries. They were effective, and were intended to be effective, only because the readers were induced to believe that the events they described had actually happened. That Jahveh could be made to do wonderful things in *mere fiction* would not have been a surprise to any Oriental, or anybody else. So the fiction was represented as fact, and the authorship was concealed under a spurious name.

We shall see presently in what sense this applies to the supposed authorship of the Pentateuch by Moses, or of the Psalms by David, or in large part of *Isaiah.* Here we will consider the Old Testament as a whole.

It professes to be, and the orthodox believe it to be, a collection of books which appeared at intervals, with divine inspiration, during a thousand years of Jewish history. It is supposed that Moses wrote, or caused to be written, the Pentateuch (except the last few verses). It is believed that *Judges, Kings,* and *Chronicles* go back to the times they describe; that the prophecies were added from the ninth century onward; and so on. Now the critical theory is that not a single book of the Old Testament, as we have it, is older than the ninth century, and that in the fifth century all the older books and fragments were combined together into the Old Testament as we have it, and were drastically altered so as to yield a version of early Hebrew history which is not true.

It is believed that this was done by the Jewish priests; and that fact, not prejudice, is the reason for the title of this chapter. The object of this manipulation of the Hebrew writings was, according to all scholars, to represent the Jewish priesthood and its rights and customs to have been established in the days of Moses. All the scholars to whom I refer admit this, and admit that the representation is false. And so, not being either a priest or a professor or other polite person, I speak of priestly forgers. You shall please yourself.

But to understand the facts we must glance at Jewish history. The next two chapters will examine the Old Testament version of that history, and I need not go into controversial details here.

The origin of the Hebrew race is obscure. What we now know is that the Arabian Peninsula generally was the cradle, the hive, of the Semitic tribes, and, owing to the great fertility of their women and the great sterility of their soil, they constantly spread from this to the north and west. The Babylonians were Semites who took over the civilization of Mesopotamia from the earlier Sumerians. No doubt Semitic tribes or families peacefully invaded the Babylonian empire, and, though the name Abraham is clearly legendary (as we shall see) it is possible that a Semitic family went from Ur, one of the oldest Babylonian cities, to distant Palestine.

What we know is that the Palestinian tribes (Moabites, Edomites, etc.) generally were Semites who had come into this relatively good country from the desert and settled there. The Hebrews are one of these tribes. They came late, found the land full, and were allowed only to settle on the poor hilly lands of what became Judea.

We know that some of these nomad tribes wandering about the desert fringe of Palestine and Egypt begged to be admitted to the outlying lands of the Delta of the Nile. Some of the Hebrew tribes may have done this. That they ever settled in Egypt proper it is difficult to believe, as there is no trace of this in the ample Egyptian remains. It is generally denied by scholars. But I should be disposed to look for some historical nucleus of the legend about the long stay in Egypt, and it may be that they were for some time in the Delta.

The earliest historical mention of them is about 1200 B.C. An Egyptian record of that time, which seems to refer to them, says that "Israalu has been vanquished." They had, apparently, settled on the fringe of Palestine, which belonged to Egypt, and were included in some chastisement of frontier tribes. Let us take it provisionally, that they had leaders called Judges, and presently kings. As to the virtues of David and glories of Solomon, we shall see later.

It is generally admitted that by the tenth century or so they were sufficiently civilized to commit some of their historical traditions and old war-songs to writing. Hebrew is the language of Canaan, and Canaan was quite civilized when the Jews arrived. It is now thought that the Philistines had brought to it the old civilization of Crete (about 1450 B.C.), and Egyptian and Babylonian culture had flowed over it for ages. It is important to remember that these were civilized more than a thousand years before anybody claims that the Hebrews were civilized. The legends and law and religions of both were well known throughout Palestine. It is, in fact, now generally held that the Hebrew written language is derived from the hieroplyphics of Egypt; though the Babylonian script was at the time also well known in Palestine. The earliest inscriptions in Hebrew are the Moab Stone (ninth century) and the Siloam Inscription (eighth century).

One of the most recent works on the subject is the *Introduction to the Old Testament* of Professor Sellin, a Berlin theologian. I am going to make much use of this, because the author is, not "advanced," but conservative. But when Professor Sellin claims that the Hebrews could write about 1300 B.C., and therefore their oldest historical traditions may have been in writing since then, I look carefully for his proofs. I find they are all from the Old Testament itself—the very book whose credibility as history is disputed. University professors ought to be more logical.

However, Professor Sellin presently enters upon a discussion of *Deuteronomy,* and we will follow him. Let me ask any religious reader to get out his Bible, and read II *Kings* xxii and II *Chronicles* xxxiv. It is there described how, about 622 B.C., "Hilkiah the priest found the book of the law of the Lord given by Moses." The priest gives it to a scribe, who reads it and takes it to the king, and reads it to him. It causes a sensation. It was so extraordinary, so remote from the actual religious life of the Jews, that the king "rent his garments"—a fearful sign of agitation in so economical a race—and then sent the priests to consult a witch (or "prophetess"), which the Bible sternly forbids. Then a crowd of the people was got together, and the strange "law" was read to them.

There seem to have been murmurs. One can imagine hard-headed Jewish merchants remarking that it was strange that the priests had so completely forgotten their own charter and rules; stranger still that their aspiring high priests should conveniently "find" it in the temple at a time when a pious and simple-minded monarch sat on the throne! In fact, read your prophet Jeremiah, the best of his class, at viii 8. As I have said, they consulted a witch, not the great Jeremiah, and these words tell you why:

> How do ye cry, We are wise, and the law of the Lord is with us? But, behold, the false pen of the scribes hath wrought falsely [in Hebrew, "a lie"].

Jeremiah, the best man of the time, saw the trick. The book was a forgery.

However, King Josiah swore very hard that, as this law was "given by Moses," they had to observe it. Rival religions, which were much patronized, were suppressed. Jahveh alone could be worshiped. His priests became enormously powerful.

This is not Higher Criticism. It is in the Bible. Candidly,

what do you think of it? The Higher Critics say that Hilkiah touched up an old law or tradition "By conflation and contamination." Strange that he knew the old law so well, yet it so much astonished even the king! Obviously, it was not in the least being carried out, though the priests knew it well enough to write it out. Professor Sellin is sure that, whatever happened, the document was not forged with the connivance of the priests; but unfortunately, he has little evidence to offer us beyond his personal conviction of this. Fundamentalists and Catholics say that it really was the law of Moses (which blazes with imprecations on those who neglect it), and it had been left for centuries in a cellar, entirely forgotten (and, of course, there was only one copy), and so far fallen into disuse that the king would not believe it until a witch confirmed it. What do *you* think?

This roll of papyrus, or whatever it was, was read by the scribe and then read by him to the king in *one day.* Apparently it was an hour, or an hour or two, of reading. The Pentateuch consists of 150,000 words, and could not be read in a day; so it was not the Pentateuch. So the Pentateuch, as we have it, did not then exist, or it would have contained this law.

The book was not even *Deuteronomy,* as we have it, for it contains 30,000 words and, as writing then was, could not be read by a scribe to a king in less than ten hours. This startling thing, a thing to be read slowly, was read twice in a day, and then at a public meeting. It was not *Deuteronomy* (which means Second Law), but—to coin a word—Proteronomy, or First Law. High priest Hilkiah had fabricated the first sketch of the rules, prerogatives, and rights of the Hebrew priesthood; and he ascribed the authorship to "Moses."

Still there was no Pentateuch—let me repeat that it would have contained this law and a good deal more—and, for reasons which we shall see in the next chapter, there could not be. Then there was a period of obscure disorder lit only by the writings called *Ezra* and *Nehemiah.* How far they light up the period. . . . Well, let us consult the conservative Professor Sellin and that redoubtable enemy of the Higher Critics Professor Sayce. Ezra and Nehemiah, Professor Sellin concludes, "were *indiffer-*

ent to, or perhaps ignorant of, the strict order of events." Is there any order of events which is not strict? Anyhow, the professor assures us that they do not tell us the truth, and, strange to say, he is quite prepared to believe that they did not care whether they told the truth or not. Professor Sayce is just as uncomplimentary to the inspired writers. They are full of errors, he says.

We shall see in the next chapter but one why even professors of the very moderate school have to say these things. The Bible contradicts the Bible, and we can have no hesitation as to which version we have to believe. We are, in fact, on the threshold of the greatest event in Jewish history, as far as this book is concerned, and the facts had to be concealed by spurious statements. The Jews were, as I said in the first chapter, deported to Babylon, and the demoralized mass of country folk who remained in Palestine, as well as the bulk of the deportees, fell away from the faith. The destruction of the temple and its priesthood meant—always did, and always will mean—that the people were free to follow their own inclination, away from religion. The priests had to make a drastic effort to bring them back.

In the year 438 Ezra, a zealous priest, returned from Babylon to Jerusalem with a party of zealots. Some years earlier a Jew named Nehemiah, who had become cup-bearer to the Persian king and had therefore much favor at court, had gone to Jerusalem and tried to restore religion, but had failed. Ezra, the priest, succeeded. He brought with him "the book of the law of Moses," and had it read to an assembly of the people, with the usual consternation and revolution in the religious life.

We must postpone the examination of the supposed historical works (*Ezra, Nehemiah,* and the uncanonical I and II *Esdras*) until the fifth chapter; but I will there show that they are forgeries perpetrated several centuries after the events. The quotations from Sellin and Sayce, given above, are mild. No scholar regards them as history; and some maintain that the entire story they tell is a fabrication, except the fact that a priestly party, headed by Ezra (in Greek Esdras), again imposed some "law of Moses" upon the people.

This law was what is known in biblical science as the Priestly code (mainly *Leviticus*). It was obviously new in Judea; and, says our reverend Professor Sellin, "in the Old Testament today its contents stand out with a peculair distinctness," so that "even the non-expert can recognize them without difficulty." It was he concludes, "worked up" in Babylon about 500 B.C. It was in its main provisions quite new to the Jews; and its plain aim was to represent the priesthood as endowed with all the rights and functions described in *Leviticus* nearly a thousand years earlier than 500 B.C. The writers, Professor Sellin thinks, used old material—he is unable to trace it, of course—and "impressed upon it the stamp of the new ideas"; that is to say, deliberately falsified history to suit their purpose.

Professor Sellin is quite sure that Ezra was unaware of any forgery. He is sure of this because *Ezra* and *Nehemiah* (which he holds to have been written *a century later,* and to be mere romances) tell us that Ezra had a great "reverence" for his book! Funny how professors write sometimes.

It is the almost universal opinion of scholars that a priestly group in Babylon, using some old material, fabricating new, and perverting the entire history of the cult and the priesthood, made this priestly code and ascribed it to Moses. Is that forgery? It is equally the almost universal opinion that in Jerusalem they went on to combine this code, again falsifying the historical facts, with the older existing writings and made the Pentateuch nearly as we have it. I give sufficient evidence of this in the fifth chapter.

As to Ezra himself, remember that he was, not only a zealous priest, but "a ready scribe in the law of Moses" (*Ezra* vii 6). In fact, for once I think we shall find much food for thought in an apocryphal work (I *Esdras* xiv 22): "I [Ezra] shall write all that hath been done in the world since the beginning and the things that were written in thy law." He (and his associates) did. The old Hebrews, admitting that he wrote the whole Pentateuch, used to say that he had "revelation" to help him. The clerical professors say that he had some mysterious fund of old materials, which he "worked up" and made to serve his purpose. What do *you* think? Remember, this book made the priesthood all-powerful for the first time in Judea.

4

The Mistakes of "Moses"

Now let us examine the Pentateuch, or "Five Books" with which the Old Testament opens. One smiles today at the vast amount of ink that was spilt in the nineteenth century over the question whether Moses wrote them. There is now no scholar who would entertain the idea. The only foundation for any belief that Moses wrote or dictated them is a statement in precisely those passages in *Kings, Chronicles,* and *Ezra*—all very late books—in which the forgers produce them and *say* that Moses wrote them. Nice evidence that!

But let us look at the first two pages from another point of view. We have already seen how absurd is the idea that if you exclude the teaching of evolution from the schools all will be well with orthodoxy. You may exclude the Higher Criticism from the colleges also, and orthodoxy is in as bad a position as ever. For the first page of the Bible is in flat contradiction to what every child now knows; and even the pious work of the Rev. Professor Sayce, issued still by the Society for the Promotion of Christian Knowledge (of a fundamentalist shade), proves emphatically that the early chapters of *Genesis* are modifications of Babylonian legends.

Attempts to "reconcile *Genesis* and science" never come now from men who know science. The Hebrew text, which I know well, having had a course of Hebrew at Louvain University, is not one inch nearer to science than the English text. It is neither poetry—I have read it in Hebrew, Greek, Latin, and English—nor accurate statement. Let us glance at it.

There is first a dark chaos, created by God. Why God created matter in a chaotic state and then, in six days, put it in order, is rather a puzle to the believer. It would be just as easy for the "creative word" to make an orderly as a chaotic universe. Desperate apologists remind you how science (which they pretend not to believe) put a nebula at the beginning; and one might (if one did not know Hebrew) think of the chaos as a nebula. But a nebula is light, not dark; and it most assuredly has no water in it. Let us use our common sense. The Hebrew for the chaos is *tohu vah bohu,* which is plainly a primitive people's corruption of the Babylonian *tiamat,* the original chaos, as we shall see. To the learned Babylonian, the first state of things was a watery waste, land and water mixed up together, and the gods had first to separate them. The Hebrew follows the Babylonian legend in all that it says.

But this is really waste of time. Any man who thinks that the teaching of science is in harmony with the *Genesis* order of creation: (1) light, (2) division of water by the sky or firmament, (3) division of land from water and creation of plants (including fruit trees), (4) appearance of the sun and moon, (5) production of birds from the water, (6) production of reptiles (after birds) and mammals and man, ought to try politics instead of theology. It is sheer nonsense. Moreover, the second chapter of *Genesis* makes matters worse by putting first the creation of man, then trees, then mammals, then woman.

It is frankly ridiculous to talk of science in such a connection. The only agreement with science (and this is undone by the second chapter) is that the grass was created before the cattle, which eat it, and the cattle before the man, who eats them. I say this quite deliberately after (for the hundredth time) reading slowly the first chapter of *Genesis.* Seriously, does one need inspiration to guess that?

Read the virtuous and admirable Sayce: the Higher Critics

do not enter this controversy. He will show you how Canaan was saturated with Babylonian culture and legends long before the Hebrews got there. And in *Morals in Ancient Babylon* (Little Blue Book No. 1076), I tell all about their legends of creation, and show how, beyond a shadow of doubt, they are the sources of *Genesis*. The primitive chaos, the coming of light first to it, the firmament dividing the waters, the late creation of sun and moon to rule the day and the night, the seven days of the week, the rest upon the seventh, the successive creations— everything is there.

Next as to chronology. I have heard fundamentalist leaders scoff at the idea that the Bible puts creation about 4000 B.C. In a debate with me Dr. Riley has said that he is quite prepared to admit that, as science claims, the earth is more than a billion years old. But if the reader cares to go through *Genesis* carefully, and note the age of each patriarch at the time his first son was born, he will find that the Old Testament does actually date creation about 6,000 years ago. I have done it. You try it.

Then there is the lovely Garden of Eden—quite plainly, we now know, the Babylonian *Edin* or plain—and the ghastly story of the curse of the whole human race for the sin of two people. It is a Babylonian story; and the Hindus, Egyptians, and others had the same story. As to Noah and the Flood, I imagine that every theologian in the world has thrown up the sponge on that wonderful specimen of early man's idea of what a God might do. It is all in the Babylonian tablets, even down to such details as the sending out of the dove and the raven and the resting of the ark on a high mountain. I quote all this in *Morals in Ancient Babylon*.

The story of Babel also is a childlike legend of which we have traces in Babylonia. It is naive enough in the Old Testament. God gets jealous of man's progress in civilization. Man has built a city, which is clearly meant for Babylon (consult the admirable Sayce), and a high tower, which means one of the lofty stepped temples of Babylonia. the whole story is a very primitive attempt to explain how men came to speak different languages.

We have today actual specimens of the Cretan, Egyptian, Meso-potamian, and Chinese languages going back ages before the alleged date of Babel.

When, in *Morals in Ancient Babylon* (Little Blue Book No. 1076) and *Religion and Morals in Ancient Egypt* ((Little Blue Book No. 1077), I describe the elaborate religions and mythologies of Babylonia and Egypt, and show how they were mighty empires before the supposed time of the Flood and how their culture spread over the entire region, all this will be fully understood. But I am not aware that any scholar, clerical or lay, of our time, questions the Babylonian origin of the *Genesis* legends, and we need not anticipate here by reproducing the ancient stories. We do not suggest that the Jews adopted these legends during the Captivity. They were probably well known in Canaan, and were, indeed, probably the only available answers to the riddle of the universe, when the Hebrews arrived there. It is probable, in fact, that they were written in a Hebrew version centuries before the Captivity. But no one can read the Baby-lonian originals, which we now have, and doubt the ultimate source of the early chapters of *Genesis.*

Properly educated clergymen admit this, and say that the "inspiration" is seen in the change from polytheism to mono-theism. The very first line, "In the beginning God created the heavens and the earth," is said to rise high above all ancient literature. But in the Babylonian legend itself it is *one* god, Marduk, who puts chaos in order and creates the world; and I show in *The Origin of Religion,* and prove more amply in *Morals in Ancient Babylon* and *Religion and Morals in Ancient Egypt* that monotheism was established in Egypt centuries before a line of the Old Testament was written.

It is precisely one of the boasts of the worthy Professor Sayce that the monuments have confirmed the existence *and monotheism* of Melchisedech, in the time of Abraham; and our other moderate professor, Sellin, remarks that, not only is the second Hebrew name for God, Elohim, a plural noun, but in some verses of the Old Testament it actually has, in the Hebrew text, a plural verb. Even in the early books of the Bible it is clear that the Hebrews did not deny the existence of other gods, but their priests restricted them—not very successfully—to the worship of Jahveh.

It is more interesting and useful to tell here what a century of analysis has brought out as regards the composition of *Genesis* and the other earlier books of the Old Testament. The name "Higher Criticism" is really wrong. The so-called critics are all clerics (and we have seen how lenient they are) and their work for more than a hundred years has consisted mainly in a literary analysis of the text. They are now all agreed on certain general conclusions which I will describe.

It is quite clear from the style and language alone that two very early writings have been used—a fragment here and a fragment there—in the compilation of the Pentateuch and early historical books. One of these calls God Jahveh (a name which no one understands, and some think a mountain or thunder god adopted by the Hebrews) and the other Elohim (the plural word "gods"). These early documents are therefore called the Jahvist and the Elohist documents.

Popular evangelical writers, always inaccuate and never having a knowledge of Hebrew, represent that it is only the two names for God which have led biblical students to distinguish two documents. As if, they say, one and the same writer might not, as we do, call the Almighty by two or three names! This is sheer ignorance. According to even Professor Sellin one of these documents was written in the tenth century B.C., the other in the ninth century, and the Old Testament as a whole compiled in the fifth century. Now think of a piece of English literature of the fifteenth century and compare it with modern English! A child could see the difference. Hence Hebrew scholars have been quite able to pick out by their style the bits of these early documents and put them together.

Well, you say, if this Jahvist wrote in the ninth or tenth century—Sellin says in the time of David—he is likely to give us some reliable facts about early history. We shall see in a moment whether he does or not. Even what he says about David is allowed only "a kernel of fact." He is valuable only as having, it is believed, preserved old songs and sayings like the Song of Lamech, the Triumphal Song of the Red Sea, the Blessing of Jacob, the Decalogue, and so on; but they must be taken as poetry, not history. It is generally said that he has preserved some reminiscence of Moses in "the Book of the Covenant"; but this is now known to be a pale reflection of the code of laws of the Babylonian King Khammurabi, as Professor Sellin admits.

These two early writings were, we can tell, combined in the eighth or seventh century. I say "combined," but the two contradictory accounts of creation in *Genesis* i and ii, the first Elohist, the second Jahvist, show how clumsily it was done. These duplications and contradictions run through two thirds of the Old Testament.

In the ninth century, as we shall see, prophets appeared, and a new sort of literature began. In the seventh century, as we have already seen, a very important new work, *Deuteronomy,* a forged version of the giving of the law and institution of the priesthood of Moses, was imposed upon the people by the priests; and it seems probable that the priests combined this with the Jahvist-Elohist work shortly before the Exile in the sixth century.

This was "the Law"; a very small book compared with our Pentateuch. But it fell into complete disuse at the fall of the Temple, and, as we saw, the group of exiled priests forged a new and larger document, making their power greater than ever and carrying back its origin to the days of Moses. This was, in the main, *Leviticus.* On their return to Jerusalem they combined this with the older writings, resolutely perverting and falsifying the whole early history so as to represent, as we now read, that Jahveh was the one God of the Hebrews from the start and that he gradually, on a deliberate plan, led them up to the complete establishment of his cult. Thus, with a few later modifications arose the Pentateuch; and Professor Sellin (who admits all this except the word "forgery") piously concludes that the Christian Church does well to retain it as "the record of the divine plan"—fabricated by a group of priests who got great profit and prestige thereby.

The "historical" works still lay apart; in fact most of them had not been written. The Samaritans who took the Pentateuch with them when they seceded from the Jews had not *Joshua*. This was the next fabrication out of ancient material (430–400 B.C.). But here we approach a new aspect of the Bible and I will turn back to what is thought to be the beginning of Hebrew history, the story of Abraham, and inquire how far the Bible contains history.

5

The Mythical History of the Jews

In popular belief the story of Abraham is very simple. His original name was Abram, and he lived in "Ur of the Chaldees"; but God called him and changed his name to Ab-ra-ham, which is the Hebrew for "the father of many peoples."

Blessed are the ignorant, for they have no difficulties. The word Abraham does not mean "the father of many peoples." No Hebrew scholar can make it mean anything. It has "no meaning in Hebrew," Dean Cheyne says. Apparently a chief named Abram was treasured in Hebrew tradition, but a later generation got confused over the name—there were then no vowels (or vowel points) in Hebrew—and spelled it Abraham. So the priestly forgers of a later date neatly joined the two together by the above story. And one trace of their handiwork is "Ur of the Chaldees." Abram may have come from Ur; but it was not a "city on the Chaldees" until ages afterwards—when the legend was written.

Abram means "high father" or "great father." Late in Jewish history he began to be regarded as the ancestor of the people. But most probably this grew out of a tradition about him, and now, say Professor Sayce and Professor Sellin, these old traditions have been gloriously vindicated and the Higher Critics shattered. New archeological discoveries have given us confirma-

39

tion of the names of certain kings mentioned in the story of Abraham. The good news spread through the religious world like a breath of spring.

This is a good illustration of the reasons why critics of the clergy and the religious press are inclined to call them dishonest. They mislead the people. Of the entire story of Abram only the fact that three or four kings mentioned are now known to have really existed is confirmed. It would follow only that there *was* an ancient legend about Abram; but of the whole *supernatural* story about him there is not a tittle of confirmation.

These supposed archeological discoveries "confirming" the Bible are all of that nature. A few names of kings, or alliances, or battles in many centuries are confirmed: a vast amount is disproved (as we saw about *Daniel*). Honest common sense will see in this only a confirmation of the view of the Old Testament which I have given. Those who fabricated it in the fifth century included some older writings which were based on tribal traditions; but what was in those writings we rarely know.

And this particular "triumph" is very modest. One of the royal names discovered is King Khammurabi of Babylon. Obviously the same name is Amraphel in the Abram story, religious writers say! It is by no means obvious; and learned Assyriologists ridicule it. Moreover, Khammurabi lived before 2000 B.C., and Professor Sellin is very much puzzled about this. However, as all that he can offer you in the end is "an ancient Canaanitish narrative which shows us Abram as a valiant Khabiri chieftain who followed the fortunes of the rules of Jerusalem," perhaps you are not further interested. The Hebrews, who came later to Canaan, appropriated the legend, made this valiant Bedouin adventurer an ancestor of their race, and the priests later decorated this scanty and bloody story with a supernatural halo.

Joseph is the next outstanding historical figure; all that lies between him and Abram is a totally unreliable "working up" of ancient legend for priestly purposes. But Joseph retires with the Khabiri chieftain into the very dim mists of ancient legend. You remember how (*Genesis* xli 43), when Joseph was set high, the Egyptian people called before him, "Bow the knee." It is now certain that this is a fanciful rendering of a word which the ancient translators did not understand. The word, we now know, is a purely Babylonian title of honor! See the worthy Sayce. Strange, isn't it, to find an Egyptian crowd talking Babylonian?

And Sayce also warns his pious reader, though very delicately, as beseems the subject, that the very popular story of Potiphar's wife has so close a parallel in an Egyptian story which we have found that it is "impossible not to see the connection." By the way, he is quite wrong in saying "impossible," for the Rabbi Dr. Jacob Horovitz in his recent attack on the Higher Critics (*Die Josephoerzahlung,* 1921) says there is no connection. You shall, as usual, please yourself. I ask only the use of common sense. Sayce himself says repeatedly that these zealots are quite as bad as the Higher Critics. "Hair-splitters," he calls both groups.

This is no new find; but it takes a long time for the discoveries to reach the body of the faithful. It was in 1852 that scholars found the Orbiney Papyrus, now in the British Museum at London. It is a story of two brothers who lived together. They were working together in the field one day, and the elder, who was married, sent the younger back to the house for some seed. The wife, who confessed she had had her eye on him for some time, saw her opportunity. "Come," she said—I am translating from Rabbi Horovitz, "let us lie together for an hour. That will be pleasant for you, and I will make fine clothes for you." The blushing youth indignantly refused, and fled: which says much for ancient Egyptian morals. So the wife, to protect herself, told people he had tried to seduce her, and, when her husband came home, she accused the younger brother of saying to her: "Let down thy hair, and let us lie together for an hour." And the elder slew the younger brother.

Well, compare for yourself *Genesis* xxxix with this. Joseph went to his master's house "to do his business," and, as there was no one else there but the wife, "she caught him by his garment, saying: Lie with me." He refused, and she turned the tables on him, as in the novel.

Do *you* see any connection? And remember the Babylonian

title and the fact that the very abundant remains of Egypt give us not the least confirmation of the story of the Jews in Egypt. Then remember how *Genesis* was put together seven hundred years later, and . . . May we not pass on?

Exodus is in exactly the same position. Sayce in fact shows that we now know that if the Hebrews had followed the route there described they would have passed through Egyptian territory! It and *Numbers* are a tissue of myths put together for a purpose centuries later. I am, as I said, inclined to believe that some of the Hebrew tribes at least entered the fringe of Egypt, and then wandered in the desert to Palestine. But their story remained oral for centuries; and the account in the Pentateuch is "a didactic novel." And *Deuteronomy* and *Leviticus* are, we saw, priestly forgeries.

Did you ever notice in the Pentateuch, which is supposed to have been written by Moses, such phrases as "the Canaanite dwelled *then* in the land" (*Genesis* xii 6 and xiii 7) or "Before there reigned any king over the children of Israel" (xxxvi 31)? All such sentences were clearly written ages after Moses: when there *were* kings in Israel, and there were *not* Canaanites. Moreover, as Professor Sellin says, "nearly every occurrence from the creation of the world to the death of Moses is related to us twice, and in some cases three times." This puts beyond the shadow of a doubt the late and composite origin. Moses, we hope, did not see his visions double.

All this runs on in *Joshua* and the other "historical books." The writer of Joshua (who never pretends to be Joshua) often says that a thing goes on "unto this day" (ix 27 and xv 63). In xxiv 31 he intimates that he is writing at least after the death of the eldest person who had known Joshua. There are the same doubles and contradictions. In short, as I said, the Samaritans know not the book; so it goes back to the fifth century, and we will waste no time on its history. Nor will we linger over *Judges,* another composite history with a purpose.

Samuel and *Kings* have all the same faults. I have quoted Professor Marti's saying how hard it is to get at the "kernel of fact" in the David story; and how other scholars deny that

there is any kernel. The plain truth is that we cannot by independent authority prove a single statement of any importance
in the history of the Jews until their history is no longer miraculous. It is a waste of time to try to get a "kernel of facts,"
and it will be far better to show in some detail that even the
latest historical works, which *ought* to be most reliable, are a
series of forgeries including, in a changed form, ancient traditions the original form of which we do not know.

We read in I *Chronicles* (xxix 7) of money being paid or
valued in *darics,* that is to say, coins of the Persian Darius;
so, obviously, this was written long after 520 (the first year of
Darius I). We read further (iii 19, etc.) that six generations had
elapsed since Zerubbabel, so the book must have been written
about 400 B.C. We read in *Nehemiah* (xii 1–26) a list of names
that go back to the time of Alexander the Great (died 323).
In a word, *Chronicles, Ezra,* and *Nehemiah* are impudent
forgeries of the fourth century, using some ancient memoirs
(perhaps—there is no proof), but giving a totally false version
of the events.

We have already seen this in the case of *Ezra* and *Nehemiah.*
Checked by the statements of the really contemporary prophets
Haggai and Zechariah, they are full of purposive misstatements.
Dean Cheyne says that "the redactors' own contributions are
largely inventions," and that this is especially true of what they
say about the return of the Jews from Babylon and the rebuilding
of the temple. Zechariah plainly shows that the exiles were still
in Babylonia when the temple was rebuilt; yet the author, or
what is politely called "the redactor," and impolitely called the
forger, of *Ezra* gives us a glowing description of 42,360 Jews,
with 7,337 servants, two hundred singing men and women, and
great troops of horse and treasures of gold. Incidentally, as we
saw in the first chapter, only about 4,000 men had been deported.
We are asked to believe that in two generations they grew, on
the fertile plains of Babylon, to 42,360; and thousands never
returned. And in those days a population took several centuries
to double!

We have, in fine, seen the value of the "history" of Ezra,

the ready scribe, bringing forward the real "law of Moses." Even the 42,360 (the nucleus of his large audience, presumably) were astonished at it. No serious scholar doubts that it was "redacted" in Babylon by the priests. "Redaction" or "recension" is the scholarly word for these things. In our own degenerate age a "redactor" would be accused of forgery if he added one line to the writings he was editing. We are asked not to give the name to priests of ancient Judea who, for their own high prophet, invented (as far as we can tell) nine lines for every one they edited, and "redacted" the one line until it became false.

But what's in a name? The main point is that practically all the experts assure you that in scores of material points the Old Testament history has been discredited, and has only been confirmed in a few unimportant incidental statements; and that the books are a tissue of inventions, expansions, conflations, or recensions dating centuries after the events. Why worry about Darwinism?

6

The Truth about the Prophets

Up to the time we have reached, the Jews had nothing that one could call a bible. In the time of David and Solomon, whose glories have departed, they may have had a lot of what we call folkore. All peoples had. Sayce says: "The fragments of Hebrew literature contained in the Old Testament are the wrecks of a vast literature which extended over the ancient Oriental world." He means the really old parts of the Old Testament which are embedded in the great tissue woven by the "redactors." Most of these stories were common to the Hebrews and all other Palestinians: legends from Babylon, stories from Egypt, folklore of Canaan, and so on. When the Hebrews learned to write, and began to write down some of them, no man can say. Probaby, but not at all certainly, in the tenth century. It is a liberal estimate. Before that they were, in the ordinary scientific meaning, barbarians, handing their stories orally from generation to generation.

Some sort of sketch of early history seems then to have been written, possibly with an introduction formed of the Babylonian legends of Creation, Eden, and Flood. It was in no sense sacred. Then "prophets" arose, and some of them wrote, or disciples wrote, their prophecies. They were not sacred writings. Then the priests "discovered" a small manual of their rights and prerogatives, and ascribed it to an ancient hero of the people named Moses, of whose real existence we cannot be sure. Anyhow, Mosaic authorship proved very impressive, and so the exiled priests, spurred to ambition by the sight of the power of Babylon and Persian priests, "discovered" a new and large law given by Moses. To this they tacked on, properly altered, the earlier and the later "histories," and the Jews had a sacred book, a bible.

This was "the Law"; and after the Law came the prophets (as well as the profits). We will make a short chapter of these. A prophet in old days was not a man who predicted, but a man who refused to call a forgery a recension. They were men who spoke out: as Jeremiah did about Hilkiah's pious fraud. They called a whore a whore, and altogether made some edifying reading for the children of British and American schools of the year 1926.

I do not object to calling a spade a spade, having some inclination that way myself, but the real modern interest in the prophets is based upon the supposition that they made remarkable predictions. These supposed predictions have been so thoroughly annihilated so long ago that it were waste of time to linger with them.

We now know enough of the character of the Old Testament to understand that a large number of the prophecies were written after the event. The prophets were "redacted," like all the other literature. Prophecies were forged during some hundreds of years. In other cases, the prophet merely referred to the past; as when Isaiah wrote some remarkable descriptions of the "Servant of God," which were for ages regarded as predictions concerning Christ, and are characterizations of Moses. In other cases the predictions were shrewd forecasts, such as we make about the weather or a baseball game; and the few cases in which the men were right have been emphasized, and the scores of cases in which they were wrong neglected. In other cases they are wrongly translated, as in the famous, "Behold a virgin will conceive"; for the Hebrew word is not "virgin," but "girl," and conception by a girl was not miraculous in ancient Judea.

No, the prophets, as distinguished from the priests, were men who spoke out; which is the real meaning of the word. But they spoke out with especial picturesqueness. The nation was young and poetic, and its ways were primitive. You remember how Saul was moved by a spirit and behaved like a dancing dervish. It was common all over that part of the ancient world: and not unknown in modern *seances.* And the prophet regarded himself as a very superior person, and was very dirty. From the prophets of Arabia, apparently, he borrowed the habit of dressing in a mantle of goat's hair and having mystic marks on his forehead.

These men (and women) were seers, and people paid them for advice. Now and again one rose to high notoriety and founded a school: probably in the wild mountains. Such was Elijah. But, alas, the moment we want to know all about him, the biblical experts intimidate us. There is, we are told, "probably a basis of fact" in the story of Elijah and Elisha, but we can't disentangle it as "the interests of the prophetic order led to some unhistoric fictions and exaggerations": not forgeries, of course. However, I am glad for once. That bear-and-innocent-little-children story always made me sick.

We may pass over these crude beginnings of the new art of prophecy and come to the great masters. Amos and Hosea were the first; and, naturally enough, they are the crudest and most poetic. A nation is most gifted with poetic imagery in its adolescence, when the imagination is far more developed than the intellect. That is why the Bible is "great literature"; at least a good deal of it is. I am not here repeating a shibboleth. I have read most of the finest poetry of many languages, and that is my opinion. It is quite natural. These parts of the Old Testament—large sections of the prophecies and early psalms, for instance—were written in the youth of the Hebrew race and translated in the youth or literary springtime of the English race.

But Amos and Hosea are morally crude in the same proportion. Amos, who seems to have been active about 750 B.C., was a shepherd. Jahveh "calls" him, and he begins to fling fiery invectives at the people; who find him his daily bread for that reason. His Jahveh is a fiercely vindictive old deity, always planning fearful schemes of punishment. The great sin is what the translators honestly call "whoredom"; which hurts the feelings of the modern professors. Judea, the one land (some think) which did not lie in darkness and the shadow of death, seems to have been full of whores, in spite of polygamy and concubinage. And, figuratively, the great collective sin of the nation is whoredom—a courting of false gods (whose existence is not denied). The Hebrews had to have monotheism drilled into them.

Hosea, who was active in the northern kingdom about the same time, or about 750 to 725, is a shade worse. The call of Jahveh to him was, he says, "Take unto thee a wife of whoredom and children of whoredom, for the land doth commit great whoredom." It seems clear, and is generally believed, that he literally obeyed the divine command, and learned to love the girl. But Israel's sins fire him, and he pours it out volcanically. It is really funny to reflect that pious people have read for centuries these scorching descriptions of the morals of Judea, yet have continued to believe that the Hebrews alone "saw the light." We know that Eygpt was then as moral as Minnesota is today, and that in Babylon they drowned people for adultery. Hosea ends, however, with a really fine bit of poetry.

Here, however, you strike a glaring instance of—are we to call it forgery, conflation, or what? The book of *Isaiah,* as we have it, is (apart from later manipulations) the work of two totally different writers, separated from each other by two centuries. It would be foolish to think that a competent Hebrew scholar cannot detect this. It is as easy as it would be to separate the parts if somebody now made a joint work out of a Massachusetts divine of the early eighteenth century and the Rev. Straton or Dr. Riley. The style, diction, and whole personality are strikingly different.

The real Isaiah seems to have been a man of good social position and education, and keenly interested in politics. He was pro-Assyrian, and he was opposed by the pro-Egyptians at court. His opponents won, and Judea cast off its allegiance to Assyria and turned to Egypt. Very well, said Isaiah, this is what you may expect; and he gave a very reasonable forecast (touched up later) of the punishment of Judea by the Assyrians. This is the extent of his "predictions."

Toward the close of the exile in Babylonia, some other Jew continued, or imitated, the prophecy of Isaiah. He "predicted" the exile; that is to say, he forged a prediction in the name of Isaiah, for the text shows when he was writing. He predicts a terrible destruction of Babylon itself (which was taken peacefully) by the Medes (who did not take it); and Babylon was in Isaiah's time not the enemy of Judea. It is quite clear that he wrote during the Captivity, but before Cyrus appeared. His language and religious ideas are quite different from those of Isaiah, but the two have been pieced together in one book. The critics politely call him Deutero-Isaiah, which means "Second Isaiah." Shall we call him the forger of half of Isaiah (thirty or forty chapters of it, including those most quoted)?

Next you take the second "major" prophet, Jeremiah. He is described as "one of the gentlest of men"; though, as we saw, he told Hilkiah in very good Hebrew that his new book was "a lie." However, Judea was still so wicked and perverse that the pessimism of the prophets touches its deepest note in Jeremiah. Generally the predictions of these prophets took the same general shape. The Jews were going to be fearfully punished—rebels generally were in those days—but the Lord would some day rehabilitate them. There is still time for the fulfillment of the latter part. Jeremiah was the son of a priest, and was "called" in the year 626.

We ought to have considered *Micah* before *Jeremiah,* as he is supposed to have been a contemporary of Isaiah. But as his work is really not worth considering (from our present point of view), and is hopelessly adulterated, we pass on to the famous Ezekiel.

The critics say that he is "far less attractive" than Jeremiah —who is the typical "dismal prophet" of all literature—so we may not be disposed to linger long in his valley of dry bones. He was a priest, of the sterner type, and was probably deported to Babylonia in 597. He spat the coldest fire that prophet ever erupted: a man of incandescent zeal for religion as a system of church-observances, but of fantastic imagery and poor diction. Nothing but a blind zeal for the "Word of God" could enable any modern person to be interested in him.

The rest of the prophets are not worth noticing. Joel ("probably the name was prefixed by the redactor [forger] out of his own head," says a learned divine), Malachi (a clumsy misunderstanding of a name, says another divine), and Obadiah ("most probably a fictitious name," says Cheyne) are fifth or fourth century forgeries. Nahum, Habbakuk, and Zehaniah are very unimporant dervishes of the seventh century. Haggai and Zechariah are genuine prophets of the sixth century, who, as we saw, prove that Esdras is a liar, as Jeremiah said. The prophets need not detain as further.

With the prophets, however, we may consider the book of Psalms. "The Psalms of David" they are called; and the writers of them repeatedly represent that they were written by King David, as in the close of Ps. lxxii. There is not a scholar in the world who now believes that any of them were composed by David. Taking advantage of the statement (which we now know to have been written centuries later) that David was "a harpist," later Jewish writers often attributed their songs to him. But internal evidence and the language itself show that they are a collection of songs or chants composed mainly five to seven hundred years after the time of David. As late as the second century B.C. it was a much disputed question amongst the Jews if David was really the author. Now everybody in Tennessee knows that he was.

The "psaltery" was a string instrument used by the Jews, and so any kind of song or hymn sung to it was called a psalm. Even the light songs composed for wedding feasts, which were very giddy occasions in the east, were sung to the psaltery; and we therefore find that some of the "psalms" (such as xiv) were simply poems to be sung at a royal marriage festival. The whole book is, in fact, merely what we should now call an "anthology" of Jewish poetry. Some psalms are taken word for word from *Samuel*. Others (such as xx, xxi, lxi, lxiii, etc.) are actually addressed to the king, and it was always quite absurd to suggest that the author of these was David or Solomon. There is only one that could possibly be considered as going back in parts to the time of David. Psalm civ is taken bodily from the Eygptian liturgy.

So we dismiss the second part of the Old Testament. The prophets and psalms are interesting as characteristic literature of a people that is just learning civilization from older nations. Some of the psalms, in particular, are so crude and bloody in their sentiments that the Church of England has lately debated in solemn conferences whether it ought not to omit them from its services. Of "inspiration" and "revelation" there is no question. They are monotheistic; but Egypt had found monotheism four or five centuries before the earliest prophet or psalmist appeared, and monotheism was a truism when the bulk of them were written.

7

Pious Fiction

We are now in a position to estimate the sincerity of the plea of those who ask us to keep the Bible in our modern schools. Sometimes they urge this because it is "great literature." Open your Bible at page one and see how far you have to read— how many days you have to read—before you come to a page that you would honestly call great literature. It is, of course, splendidly rendered, in fine poetic old English; but only certain parts of it, chiefly in the Prophets and the Psalms, are really fit to help in forming a literary taste, and those parts are for adults, not children. This plea is not sincere.

But it is usually said that the Bible is invaluable as a unique record of the evolution of a people and its religion. We now realize how insincere this is. The men who make the plea are precisely those who reject the "inspiration" of the Bible—or they would not plead for it in this way—and are aware of the results of critical work. They know well that the order of the books in the Bible is as far as possible from a chronological order, and that the story of the religious evolution of the Jews which the Old Testament in its present form tells is a priestly forgery. The facts were quite different.

The reader may find it useful if I sum up for him the real chornological order of the Old Testament, as far as we have now analyzed it. The first books (but touched up later) are *Amos* and *Hosea*. It is possible that the Jahvist and Elohist narratives which are blended in the early books are just as old, if not a little older, but you would have to consult the learned works of biblical experts to get these more or less in their original form. Even then they are merely very unsafe tribal traditions, such as we find in all nations at that stage of development, with a preface consisting of old Babylonian legends about the early history of the world; and they are now lost in a tissue of priestly fabrications of the fifth century, and have been deliberately falsified in what they say about early religion.

Then you may take *Samuel* and *Judges—Kings* and *Chronicles* you must relegate almost entirely to a later date—but you must still remember that there is only "a kernel of fact" in the various stories. *Jeremiah, Micah,* and the real *Isaiah* (if you can pick him out) come next; and you find yourself as far as the Babylonian Captivity with only as much real history, especially of religion, as would fill ten pages of the Bible. *Ezekiel,* the second *Isaiah, Haggai, Zechariah,* and the crowd of unimportant minor prophets and many of the psalms cover the next stage; but by that time you are in the great age of forgeries, and you must go warily.

The truth is that it is particularly difficult to trace the religious development of the Hebrews. Who Jahveh originally was, or what the name means, there is no agreement whatever. It is quite generally agreed that the Hebrews were at first polytheistic—some think they had human sacrifices—but we cannot say when they became monotheistic. Their story has been too zealously "redacted." In any case, the transition was very gradual and slow, the priests taking centuries to tear the people away from their popular "high places" and Palestinian gods. Phallic elements were very pronounced in their religion. All that we know for certain is that in the sixth and fifth centuries the priests made two resolute campaigns, mainly relying on forgeries, and created the religion of Jahveh as the Old Testament at present, and quite falsely, reflects it.

But this is never the final stage. As I say in *The Origin*

of Religion (Little Blue Book No. 1008), the facts of human evolution quite plainly tell us that the normal and universal development is: spirit-belief, animism, polytheism, monotheism, and atheism. The Jews, before their national existence was destroyed, never became sufficiently advanced in culture to reach the last stage, but the later books of the Old Testament show how they were approaching it. Babylonian and Egyptian influence had given them cosmic legends, monotheism, and an elaborate priesthood and ritual. Now Persian and Greek influence began; and the Jews got as far as "wisdom books," with much skepticism.

Many of these later books are just pious fiction, with or without a purpose. *Ruth,* which is put amongst the historical books, was written centuries after the events it describes. The writer quite openly professes to tell a story of remote days, and the language and general atmosphere and blunders about old names indicate that he lived about the end of the sixth century. After the return of the Jews from exile one of the burning questions was marriages with foreign women, and this "topical" story was written as part of the controversy.

Job has troubled commentators in all ages. Even the early critics were puzzled about its aim, as there is really no solution of the problem of evil in the book. We now see that there is no purpose at all, as the book does not come from a single writer. Like Topsey, it grew: it was not made. The original nucleus, or group of speeches, seems to have been written about 500 B.C., and additions were made to this for the next two centuries. The first author seems to have been an Egyptian Jew, and so in a position to write freely about God. Even the old rabbis often held that there was no such historical person as Job. The curious name Job seems to be an ignorant corruption of the name of the Babylonian "Adam," Ea-bani.

Daniel and *Jonah* we have already seen to be mere pieces of pious fiction. *Tobit* and *Judith,* which are in the canon of the Roman Catholic Bible, are in the same class.

I remember well the nervousness and fear of the higher authorities with which Catholic scholars began, forty years ago, to ask if *any* errors could be admitted in the Old Testament.

Even the learned Cardinal Newman solemnly asked: Are we bound to believe as an historical fact that Tobit's dog wagged its tail as is stated in the book? We now see clearly that *Tobit* was written, probably in Egypt, only about a hundred years before Christ! *Judith* was written about the same time. The writer has scarcely even an elementary knowledge of the period he deals with, and in this case the critics generally do not profess to find so much as "a kernel of fact."

The first book of *Maccabees,* also in the Catholic Bible, is a fairly honest late history; the second book a quite untrustworthy work written after the death of Christ. The books of *Esdras* (of the Catholic Bible) are fictitious continuations of *Chronicles,* and even worse.

Esther, a very popular book in the Protestant world, suggests curious reflections on human nature. The morality of the book is abominable. Esther is the ancient Oriental woman at her worst: crafty and vindictive. The vengeance of the Jews would, if it were true, be one of the most shocking episodes in the Old Testament: which is saying much. I calculate that the author makes the Jews slay, in sheer revenge, about 100,000 Persians.

But the historian has even more to say than the moralist on such matters as this, and he pronounces the book a clumsy forgery of the second century. The language of the author and his complete ignorance of Persian life—as Persian scholars tell us—confirm this. The names are ridiculous, and the supposed events are a tissue of "improbabilities and impossibilities." Again the critics despair of finding a "kernel of fact." But as the author pretends that he is writing authentic history (see the last verse but one), we have no option but to put him amongst the forgers.

Next we have a group of books, *Ecclesiastes, Ecclesiasticus,* and *Wisdom* (the latter two in the Catholic canon), which reflect the coming of Greek influence. *Ecclesiastes* is one of the strangest books that was ever included in a sacred collection. The author is an Epicurean philosopher. He believes in God, but is an Agnostic as to a future life. Over and over again he expresses his skepticism, so that the one verse which does profess belief in a future life is palpably part of the retouching which (as we can trace) the book suffered later at orthodox hands. The writer disdains the temple sacrifices (v 1) and constantly urges his readers to eat and drink and be merry while the sun shines. He was probably a Jew living in the new Greco-Egyptian city of Alexandria about 200 B.C. We will not call him a forger, as his assumption of the name of Solomon would deceive nobody.

Proverbs is much earlier, probably going back to the fourth century, when Greek influence began, but the *Wisdom of Solomon,* or *Ecclesiasticus,* is a work written in Greek in the first century before Christ by (probably) another Alexandrian Jew. It has, significantly, no hope of a Messiah; but it has plenty of Greek philosophy, which was not born until five centuries after Solomon.

But the most curious and entertaining book of the whole Bible and one of the finest and most genuine pieces of literature in it, is the *Song of Solomon.* I used to blush when, as young students for the priesthood, we solemnly chanted its voluptuous verses about ladies' thighs and breasts and bellies. We were told that it was all a superb symbol of the union of Christ and his Church, or at least the union of Jahveh and the synagogue. Even in the prudent translation which we have in the Bible it is what we should call, if it were *not* in the Bible, a most licentious piece of work, and we should call the attention of the police to it.

We are not at all sure that there is not a mythological element in parts of it, which seem to celebrate the union of the sun-god and moon-goddess (Shelamith). But as a whole it is plainly a collection of Oriental marriage songs. In the east a marriage festival lasts a week, and songs about the charms of the bride and bridegroom's particular interest in her are features of the celebration. Some of these songs may be quite old, but others include Persian, and even Greek, words, so that the collection must belong to about the fourth century. By that time the forged historical works had made Solomon and all his glory and his wives very popular amongst the Jews, and an aspiring author could not do better than borrow his name. As far as we can recover traces of Solomon through the mists of time—a petty king living in a third-rate Oriental mansion—he was quite capable of writing this (though not quite in such grand language) about a young lady's "navel" and "belly" and so on. We bowdlerize *Hamlet,* where the prince talks to Ophelia; and we read solemnly to our children from the *Song:* "He shall lie all night betwixt my breasts," etc.

8

Conclusion

That is the true Old Testament. Let me conclude with just a word about the Higher Critics. I have here and there in this book poked a little fun at these Higher Critics for the timidity with which they invent polite and obscure words where the word "forgery" best meets the case. One understands their position. In part they depend upon the less educated body of the Churches —all are ministers of religion and clerical professors—and in part they genuinely shrink from injuring what they call "real religion" by too outspoken a description of the way in which the Bible was imposed upon the world.

But I have a great admiration for these scholars, and I would suggest to any religious reader that, when he prefers the violent and ignorant language of some very poorly educated preacher to their most learned and conscientious labors, he is playing with truth. I have, in this short space, crowded enough of their literary analysis of the Old Testament to show any person that it is solid, scientific, indisputable work. Paine and Ingersoll, both still well worth reading, made a common-sense analysis of the Old Testament. Even their work is indisputable. But all the resources of learning—philology, archeology, and history— have since been applied, by sincere Christian scholars, to a deeper analysis, and common sense still approves the work and the conclusions. The Higher Critics are very learned men: their critics are very far from being learned men. Common sense tells you what to do, if you care about the truth of *your* opinions.

But I have shown sufficiently that the Bible, properly read, itself exposes its weaknesses. We ought now to pass to the New Testament. For that, however, and to complete our understanding of the Old Testament, we need more knowledge of the great civilizations which educated Judea and prepared the way for Christianity. In *Morals in Ancient Babylon, Religion and Morals in Ancient Egypt,* and *Life and Morals in Greece and Rome* (Little Blue Books Nos. 1076, 1077, and 1078), we survey this ancient world and learn the surprising discoveries which have in recent years entirely altered our estimate of it.

The Myth of Immortality

1

The Law of Death

In *The Origin of Religion* (Little Blue Book No. 1008) I defined religion, which is the general theme of this series, as the belief in and worship of gods.

If there is any error in that definition, it is that it ignores the belief in immortality. That man's mind survives the body is, in fact, as we saw, the oldest of all religious beliefs, the germ of all religious thought. Gods were but the princes of the spirit-world. God is its monarch. What if the spirit-world became, like the human world of which it is a fantastic imitation, a republic without aristocracy or princes? Could we have religion without god?

One would expect men to cling more desperately to the belief in immortality than to the belief in god, yet in that universal decay of religion which I have described there is as much indifference to the disappearance of the one as of the other dogma. Did men ever profoundly believe in their immortality?

The logic of theology is nowhere more inexorable than in this section. If we are to live three score years and ten on earth, and an eternity in some other sphere, it matters vitally how we prepare for that larger life. And the majority of men have always behaved as if they did not entirely believe the story. The flesh, and its impulses and pleasures they knew, but that dim far-away crown. . . .

Yet at a time when even the dimmest vision of the crown seems to fade, when the rumor spreads that heaven is an illusion, one would think that the most earnest efforts would be made to save the hope. No. Few but professional theologians concern themselves with it. Hardly one in ten of our more learned men now believes in personal immortality, and the news passes from ear to ear. And not a tear falls: not the thinnest shade clouds the inconquerable gaiety of modern life. The angelic harp is the butt of our comedians. Hell is the text of humorous stories.

And the official reply to all this is remarkably feeble. Every man who believes in god has one or another reason for doing so always present in his mind. God must have made the world, or at least the order and beauty of the world, or must have laid down the moral law. But ask your religious neighbor why he believes that he is immortal. The answer will be a series of gasping exclamations: "Why-er, surely-er." And so on. I venture to say that not one believer in a thousand has in his mind one single definite reason for thinking that he is immortal.

Most people will candidly reply that they believe because the Bible says so, or the Church says so. Since the Church can say so only on the authority of the Bible, we are reduced to that. And to accept such authority with any confidence in the truth of your belief, you must first be quite convinced, by solid proof, that there is a god to make the promise, and that he actually did inspire the Bible. In *The Futility of Belief in God* (Little Blue Book No. 1060) I show how frail is the belief in the very existence of god, and another volume shows that the claim of revelation in the Bible (whether there is a god or not) is far frailer.

It is strange how people forget that religion is a series of statements of fact, and the boldest and most tremendous statements imaginable. Perhaps the reader will be surprised to know that it is profoundly difficult—many thinkers say impossible—to prove the existence of the material world; of your body and the house you live in. Religion makes the far more formidable statement that there is a Power beyond and greater than the world. But in claiming that man is immortal it makes an even more astounding statement, and one for which we require very clear and cogent proofs.

Death is the law of the universe. In the days when Plato worked out the first rational arguments for immortality, as distinct from mere religious tradition, the claim was not so exorbitant. The stars themselves, the Greeks thought, were immortal. They were small, undying fires set in the firmament. Plants and animals died, of course, but these stars made men familiar with things which never died.

Now we know that the stars—not three thousand of them, as the Greeks thought, but two billion—are born and grow and die just like dogs, except that their life is immeasurably longer. There is a time when each is a shapeless cloud of stardust. There will be a time when the most brilliant star in the heavens will fade from the eyes of whatever mortals there may then be. They are made of the same material as our bodies: of gas and earth and metal. They fall under the great cosmic law that things which come together shall in the end go asunder—shall die.

A hundred years ago a few religious men of science, trying to help theologians to reconstruct belief, said that, while stars were certainly not immortal, the atoms of matter of which they were composed never changed and never died. An atom of carbon or of oxygen, they said, is an article "manufactured" (or created) once for all. There is no dissolution for it.

They were wrong, as everybody now knows. Atoms are composed of tinier particles called electrons. They break up into these electrons. In the hottest stars very few of our atoms are as yet formed. And now astronomers tell us that the stars may entirely burn themselves out, so to say, and leave not an atom behind. Matter may change into "energy." I would not here press my own opinion, but I believe that it will eventually be found that matter is evolved out of ether and in the star much of it may return to ether. The electrons, I think, are centers in ether and may dissolve into it.

In that case, you may say, ether is immortal. Probably it is. As I said in *The Futility of Belief in God,* men of science now generally regard the universe as eternal, and it is only the ultimate and fundamental material of it, the ether, which shows no beginning and no end. That does not help the belief in human immortality, however. Man is the most complex thing in the universe, and the law of death is that all *complex* things return sooner or later into their elements. It is a law of universal dissolution.

If I cared to indulge my imagination, to let my pen weave pretty patterns of words, as Theosophists, Hindoo mystics, preachers, and poets do, I could make out a good case for this law of death. Nature, one might say, thus gives a chance to countless myriads of things to enjoy their hour of life. The stuff which made a star of a quadrillion years ago now shines in Arcturus or Aldebaran. The matter of which the brontosaurs and cycads were compacted in the earth's Middle Ages is now molded into horses and palms. We humans have our chance because the living things of long ago died and left the matter of their bodies to be used in new forms.

But it is precisely the aim of these Little Blue Books to put readers on their guard against such verbiage. Let us reason only with facts. The law of the universe is death. The day dies, as I write this, and will never return. The stars on which I shall presently look, the flowers of the spring toward which I sail, the nearest animals to man in nature, all die. Spiritualist prattle about the immortal souls of cows and cats is too frivolous to be considered here. The law is death.

You say that you are an exception to this universal law. Your body will dissolve into its elements, but *you* claim to be immortal. Your "soul," you say, is not compacted of different elements, and will not be dissolved into elements.

I am quite prepared to consider it; only, reflect, you must now give stronger proofs than were ever required before. "Why," you may ask, "must I? Why should I give any proofs at all?" There was a brilliant American (ultimately British) novelist, Henry James, who believed in personal immortality, and he one day told the world why he believed. "Because I choose to," he said. He knew that he could not prove it.

Possibly many people believe because they choose to, and,

since the whole of this series of booklets is concerned with supposed proofs of religious statements, let us have a word on this point.

When you say that you believe because you choose to, what do you mean by "believe"? The usual meaning is to accept a statement as true. But to accept a statement as true without proof is impossible, unless you take it on the authority of others. All that you can mean is that you will go on repeating the statement because you like to. It may be a pretty statement. It may soothe your mind. You may be indifferent as to whether it is true or not. But it is psychologically impossible for you to believe it to be true without proof or authority, and I am not concerned with people who repeat creeds and care not whether their statements be true or false.

So we are concerned here only with the proofs of the statements they make. The law of the entire universe is death, and you state that one single being in it, man, one amongst myriads of living things on a single globe out of myriads of globes, is a grand exception to the law. I ask proof in proportion to the magnitude of the claim.

But, you will say—and this is the nearest approach to an argument that most people could offer—man is so obviously different from everything else in the universe that the claim really has a plausible ground. Man builds cities, writes poems, measures the universe. Does any other creature in the world even remotely approach him in his powers and his nature?

There is certainly one human power which is remarkable and convenient: the power of generalizing. Remember that in reality there is no such thing as "man." There are only men. Now which man do you mean? I presume that *you* do not build cities, write poems, or measure the universe. A few men do these things. But—

But, you say, there is a perfect gradation of power from me to these intellectual aristocrats of the race. It is only a question of degree. I have the same nature as they.

Yes, quite true, and it cuts both ways. The sodden, stupid brute in the gutter has the same nature as you. The laborer, so low in intelligence that he cannot even understand what other men discover, has the same nature. The Negro in the forests of the Congo has the same nature. The wild Veddah in the forests of Ceylon has the same nature. Are they so mightily different from the other forms of life?

In fact, not so long ago there were no men who could write poems or measure the universe. Consider the whole race as it was a hundred thousand years ago, and we know it well. Men could not even make homes of the rudest description. They had not begun to scratch the outline of an elephant on a bone or a stone. The utmost that any man could do was to chip a piece of flint a little better than his neighbor.

And this is by no means the lowest level of humanity that is known to us. On the contrary, man was then already some millions of years old. We can trace him to half a million years ago. There is no savage in the world so low as the entire race then was. Suppose some glimmer of the philosophic spirit had then arisen in the dull brain of one of these early prehistoric humans. Suppose he had announced to his fellows that they were so vastly superior to all the rest of the living world that they must be immortal. I fancy that these squat, hairy, beetle-browed predecessors of ours would have smiled their first smile.

You see the fallacy. A few men can do wonderful things, and we naturally claim the credit for "man": which includes ourselves. But even we, though most of us are not very obviously spiritual and immortal beings, are certainly evolved from a lower type, which looked still less spiritual and immortal. From this we go back to a still earlier type of man, so brutal and animal-like that the claim of a spiritual and immortal nature really begins to be grotesque. And, finally, we go back even beyond this type and we see the most primitive semblance of humanity merging into the "lower animal" type from which, you say, we are so glaringly different that you can claim for man the unique privilege of deathlessness.

In other words, the one reason which most people have in their minds for claiming immortality is quite unsound. The ordinary and unanimous teaching of modern science has, I will not say undermined, but annihilated it. But Professor Osborn, you may remind me, is a great authority on prehistoric man, and he has solemnly assured us that there is no conflict between evolution and religion.

Well, let us see the facts, and you may draw your own conclusion. In *The Futility of Belief in God* I show how evolution concerns very seriously the question of the existence of god. We shall now see that it has an even more destructive effect upon the doctrine of immortality.

2

Evolution and the Soul

Scientific men—the few scientific men—who assure you that there is no conflict between science and religion mean between *their* science and *their* religion—not yours. And these men generally know as little as the general public does about those branches of science which chiefly concern us when we talk of such a conflict. Professor Pupin,* for instance, is a mathematician, and we agree that mathematics does not conflict with theology. Professor Millikan† is a physicist, and physics also has no point of contact with religion. They both speak in the name of sciences which they do not know. Sir Oliver Lodge, a physicist, is in the same position.

The case of Professor Osborn,‡ the self-constituted loud speaker of American science, is different. He says that he is a Christian, though not a Christian in the meaning of any Christian Church, of course. Creation of Adam, Eden, Fall, Deluge, Atonement for original sin—he pooh-poohs the lot of them. What exactly he does believe he is too discreet to say. But, after all, religion is generally understood to include a belief

---

*Michael Idvorsky Pupin (1858–1935). (Ed.)

†Robert Andrews Millikan (1868–1953). (Ed.)

‡Henry Fairfield Osborn (1857–1935). American paleontologist. (Ed.)

in the immortality of the soul, and, when Professor Osborn, who is an authority on the evolution of man, assures the world that there is no conflict between the statements of science and the statements of the Christian religion, we will asume that he is not ignoring the one branch for which he is entitled to speak.

Let us see. It is the settled and unanimous teaching of many branches of science—anatomy, physiology, psychology, archeology, anthropology—that man was evolved from a common ancestor with the apes. I am not going to prove this here. These Little Blue Books are for serious people: not for men who imagine that Mr. Bryan* or Dr. Riley, to say nothing of the average fundamentalist preacher, really knows better, on a point of science, than all the experts in the world. That is a humorous, not a serious, attitude. Science most decidedly teaches, without a single dissenting voice today, officially, that man, body and mind, was evolved.

To appreciate properly the bearing of this on religion, let us put it in a more or less narrative shape. Long ago, in what geologists call the early Miocene Period, which was between ten and twenty million years ago, there were man-like apes in Europe and Asia. We find their bones in undisturbed Miocene deposits.

Now, since it is certain that they and man had a common ancestor, the human branch of the family must then have been in existence. Professor Osborn is fond of saying, with great fervor, that science does not teach that man comes from an ape. But a higher authority, Professor Elliot Smith, says precisely the opposite, and he is right. If we found the skeleton of the common ancestor, we should certainly classify it as a new ape, and it is highly probable that if we found the skeleton of the semihuman cousin of the Miocene apes we should call it an ape. It would be something like, but inferior to, the Taungs ape, discovered in South Africa a year ago.

---

*William Jennings Bryan (1860–1925). Bryan was one of the prosecuting attorneys, in the notorious "Monkey" trial of 1925, against Tennessee high school teacher John T. Scopes, who taught evolution in defiance of state law. (Ed.)

How do we know this? Because the earliest traces of man which we have are millions of years later than the early Miocene Period—the time when the family split—yet these remains themselves are singularly ape-like. If the reader knows the Java remains and the Piltdown skulls and the Heidelberg jaw, the earliest human bones, only from pamphlets or books written by men like Riley, McCann, or Mauro, he must not try to persuade himself that he knows anything about them. The Java creature is admittedly half-ape, half-man. The Piltdown and Heidelberg jaws are now beyond all controversy.*

My point is that on the accepted and unanimous teaching of science man took several million years to evolve from the ape to the ape-man stage. He then took a few hundred thousand years to evolve from the ape-man to the savage-man stage. You may say that you do not believe it. I admire your courage, but the present question is merely whether science unanimously and officially teaches this. I had in the winter of 1925–1926 seven debates with fundamentalist leaders, and I challenged them to name one single living scientific authority who dissented. They could not—in my presence. No doubt they did when I was far away.

A child could see the bearing of this on the belief that man has a spiritual and immortal soul. The ape has no such spiritual principle. Then at what stage in this long and gradual evolution was an immortal soul infused into the developing body? Do you think the Java ape-man had an immortal soul? If so, can you suggest any reason whatever why this transcendent mental principle of his took three or four hundred thousand years to raise the race to the level of the Australian black?

No one, I imagine, will seriously claim it. Ten or more million years of evolution are surely enough to account for a rise from the ape-level to the ape-man level. We can reconstruct this Java

---

*"Piltdown man," discovered in 1912, was supposed to show the link between human beings and apes; the Piltdown cranium was, however, revealed as a hoax in 1953. Yet this in no way invalidates the truth of evolution. Today there are many laboratory and field tests for authenticity, which would preclude the possibility of such a fake's being accepted as genuine. (Ed.)

man quite confidently. We have his thigh bone, two of his teeth, and—most important of all—the upper part of his skull, the brain case. No savage ever known was nearly so low as he. And if you are very desperate, and suggest that, after all, this semi-human being may have had an immortal soul, because he was higher than the orang, what about the Taungs ape? This is probably not in the line of man's ancestry, nor is, for that matter, the Java man. That makes no difference. They show that evolution can carry things far above the ape-level.

But you probably give up to the crouching bestial human of ancient Java. Well, what about Piltdown man? A mistake was made at first in reconstructing the battered skull, but it is now rectified, and we have found a second skull at Piltdown. We have also found a jaw near Heidelberg of much the same age—three or four hundred thousand years ago—and type.

This was the European race, the highest known, of a quarter to a half million years ago. Examine any good reconstruction of it—not the one still retained by Professor Osborn in the Hall of Man at the New York Natural History Museum, which is five years out of date—and ask yourself seriously whether it really required the infusion of an immortal soul to raise the ape-man from the level of this very ape-like beast.

To be accurate, Piltdown man is not more advanced beyond the Java man than the latter is beyond the orang. Therefore, if natural evolution can account for the one advance, it can account for the other.

People so often forget the common-sense principle in these matters that I will repeat it. The evolutionist has not to prove that evolution could make man. It is the anti-evolutionist or creationist who must prove that it could not. I have already said why. The essential basis of the religious argument is that evolution does not suffice and *therefore* we must postulate a god or a soul.

Let us see where we are, then. Evolution has brought us from the common ancestor of ape and man to the ape-like human of a quarter of a million years ago, and I know no one who seriously wonders if these men of a quarter of a million years ago really had an immortal soul. The fundamentalist attitude is to deny the facts. That sounds easy, when you do not know the evidence, though personally I have never elicited from any fundamentalist spokesman any plausible reason why all the experts in the world should be wrong and he right.

From this human level of a quarter of a million years ago to the Beethovens and Shakespeares of the race the gradual evolution is so well known that I do not see how anyone can find a stage in which he would claim the infusion of an immortal soul: a soul which never knew its own existence until, long afterwards, it began to speculate childishly on the shadow of the body or its reflection in water. (See *The Origin of Religion*— Little Blue Book No. 1008.)

By this time man had begun to chip flints and give them a rough cutting edge. The first thing he learned to do, when he became intelligent enough, was to brain his neighbor. Anyhow, these stone implements reflect the intelligence of early man as faithfully as if he kept a diary through the ages. And the gradual rise of them during a quarter of a million years is portentously slow and never shows a sudden advance. We should surely expect so tremendous an event as the infusion of an immortal soul to break the monotonously slow advance somewhere and give us an appreciable rise!

There is no such thing. Those stone implements, representing several hundred thousand years of human life—we have millions of them—put the gradual evolution of the human mind beyond question. Alfred Russel Wallace was the last man of science to question it, and he had no knowledge of prehistoric science, and merely acted in the interest of his spiritualist beliefs. Amongst the experts on the subject the evolution of the human mind was settled thirty years ago.

But I am forgetting a rather consoling piece of news which Professor Osborn gives the believer. Many years ago we found certain human bones at Cro-Magnon in France, and the skulls were remarkably large. The brain of these representatives of some lost race of about twenty thousand years ago was larger than that of the average European of today! They were a race of geniuses, says the professor. If you could put their sons besides yours on the benches at Columbia or Chicago University, they would take all the prizes. And so on.

Well, this sounds promising. Does Professor Osborn draw the conclusion that here a spiritual and immortal soul was infused into man? He does not go so far. For a good Christian he is singularly shy of creations. He merely says that this is a case of "emergent evolution." What, you ask, is that? and I can only reply that it is a pretty phrase coined by another religious scientist, Principal Lloyd Morgan.

Seriously, we need not go into this emergent evolution because Professor Osborn does not understand the simple facts about this "Cro-Magnon race." He does not seem to know that they were exceptionally tall men, more than six feet high. The brain generally is the dynamo of the body. It is only the thin film of nervous tissue over the forepart of it that is the organ of intelligence. As a matter of fact, we have the tools, weapons, and decorations of these Cro-Magnon men. They are at about the same level as those of the Eskimo. Moreover, European ethnologists assure us that the Cro-Magnon type of head is still common in northern Spain and southern France: amongst the stupid peasants, not the aristocracy. The Cro-Magnon genius is a clumsy myth.

This is no place to tell all the facts, but the reader may care to know how it is that such a myth could arise. The truth is that twenty or thirty thousand years ago the European race was advancing rather rapidly in comparison with its advance of the previous ten million years. Do not misunderstand. Man's progress even then was enormously slower than it is today. Moreover, we quite understand the quickening of the pace. Man was in the throes of his struggle with the Great Ice Age. You must read elsewhere all that that meant for man. It led to articulate speech, clothing, social life, and a hundred new things.

There was also a great deal of shifting of population. Races appear suddenly in Europe and we do not know where they were developed. But we have today a very good knowledge of the period, and there is no mystery. We might say that the difference between the mental level of the Cro-Magnon invader and the old European is much like that between an American engineer invading Mexico and a Mexican. People do not exactly claim that a new immortal soul has been created, or that there has been an "emergent" evolution out of the abyss of religious mystery, to explain that difference.

No, there is not a single page in the chronicle of man on which you can put your finger and say: here the power of a god intervened, or here a supremely new and higher principle appears in man. From the lowest ape-like level to the highest known, from Miocene animalism to twentieth-century civilization, it is an entirely human and natural story of evolution. The most rapid advance every made in the history or the race has been in the last one hundred years.

It would be too ironical to claim that man became gifted with a soul just when he came to disbelieve in it! But we moderns have made more mental progress in a century than the race ever before made in a millennium. Do not be misled by the brilliance of a score of Greeks two thousand years ago. The *race* has made far more progress in our time. Do not listen to essayists who tell you that the race has made no mental progress since twenty thousand years ago. They are thinking of the myth of the Cro-Magnon race. *Ours* is the great age of advance— and of materialism.

But that is another story. For the moment our case is complete. Evolution makes the belief in an immortal soul improbable in the last degree. It does not disprove it. We do not attempt to prove negative statements. But, clearly, we now, in face of the general law of death and man's continuity with the animals, demand very strong and clear proof of the religious claim.

3

Is the Mind a Spirit?

Many readers will be impatient of the caution, the reserve, the timidity, with which I draw my conclusions. If man's mind is but a gradual evolution of the mind of the ape, why not say outright that the myth of the soul has been disproved? If there is no serious evidence for God in nature or in the mind or the heart of man, while there is so much that excludes the idea of a divine ruler, why not declare bluntly that you are an atheist?

I have said why. Materialism—which means that matter alone can exist, and therefore that spirit does not exist—and atheism are dogmatic negations. I do not like dogmatic negations. The old Scottish jury verdict "Not proven" seems to me the more rational attitude. But on this question of the soul there are strong reasons for hesitating, and we must see these first.

The brain is the organ of the mind. We all admit that. A genius or an idiot is a man with an abnormal brain. The mind, a believer might say, can express itself only according to the quality of its organ or instrument. Paderewski himself could not make perfect music with a hundred-dollar piano. So we may suppose that the spiritual and immortal soul was there all the time, but it could not express itself until the organ was perfectly developed.

A very sound principle—in the abstract. It is conceivable

that mind is a spiritual artist using a material instrument. Luther Burbank has said somewhere that Mr. Bryan, of whom he was a personal friend, has a "skull which visibly approached the Neanderthal type." So the many foolish things Mr. Bryan said may have been due only to the imperfectness of his mind's instrument. The mind may be the same, all the time, in everybody. It may be merely the brain that differs, from age to age, and in different individuals now.

All this is conceivable; in fact, we may find it useful in the next chapter. But the religious person must think clearly what he is saying. When does he suppose that god created the immortal mind of man? He might as well put the great event in the Miocene Age, since there is no other time more suitable. Well, we have not only seen that there probably is no god to create a soul, but even granting that there is, the whole thing remains a painful mystery. Why create the soul millions of years before it can act? Why go on creating souls—for the only plausible theological theory is that the soul has to be created in each individual human being—during those millions of years of the lowest savagery? Not very plausible, is it?

Moreover, let us reflect for a moment on this musical instrument idea. Sir Oliver Lodge is very fond of using this figure of speech, and it is as superficial as most of his work in the field of religion. Preachers find it most impressive. The brain is merely the organ, the piano, the violin, the harp. The soul is the musician.

A figure of speech is useful only if it helps you to understand something. Now this musical instrument idea only helps you to understand the relation of mind and body by *assuming precisely the point which you have to prove.* That point is whether the mind is a spirit, and the action of the musician's mind on the piano does not help us in the least unless we suppose, to begin with, that it is a spirit. If, as many hold, the mind is only a function of the brain, then it is a question of the action of matter (brain and muscle) on matter. It illustrates nothing.

In any case, even on religious principles, the mind does

not play on the body. It is one with the body. They make a composite being of the most intimate nature. There is not the least analogy with the musician, who can close his piano and leave it when he likes. The "analogy" is just a slipshod superficial substitute for accurate thinking.

To return, however, to our point. We all admit that the brain is the organ of the mind. The materialist says that the mind is merely a function of the brain, and there are quite brilliant scientific men, such as Dr. Chalmers Mitchell or the late Professor Loeb,* who say this. The believer in immortality—the spiritualist in the proper sense of the word—says that mind is a spirit which uses brain as its organ.

It has always been an insoluble problem in religious philosophy how a spirit can act on or through matter. I do not want to press this, but the reader who is inclined to think that "god" and "soul" explain things ought to be reminded of it. No thinker who ever lived has given us the least plausible idea how spirit can act on or with matter. It merely introduces new mysteries instead of "explaining" the mystery of thought.

So again, and for the third time, we have a reason for demanding that the proofs of the spirituality of the soul shall be particularly strong. There is a strong presumption against it: (1) because death is the rule of the universe, (2) because man's mind is certainly evolved from a mind that is not spiritual and immortal, and (3) because it is unintelligible and creates more mysteries than it solves. And we shall see further reason in the next chapter.

But a presumption against a statement is not a disproof of it. Let us be open-minded and logical. Practically all philosophers hold that the mind is a spirit. Why?

By the way, it occurs to me that the believer will have a sudden gush of joy on reading the preceding sentence. For once, he will exclaim, I have "practically all" the experts on my side, because philosophers are experts in this matter. But the point is not so important as it may seem. In the first place, half these

---

*Jacques Loeb (1859–1924). American biophysiologist. (Ed.)

philosophers say that the natural world does not exist. Do you follow them in that? In the second place, very few of them believe in personal immortality. I am sorry to discourage hope, but philosophy (of which I was once a professor) is a dangerous ally to invoke.

Let us first see what we mean by spirit. I hope I have many religious readers, and I invite them frequently just to reflect on what they mean. What do you mean by spirit? How does it differ from matter? I have had a very large experience in asking this question, and I scarcely ever got a coherent answer to it. Nine-tenths, at least, of the preachers and essayists who tell the world that its future depends entirely on cultivating the spirit and avoiding materialism could not tell you what spirit is. Spiritual books always forget to define it.

The religious philosophy which I taught thirty years ago was clear enough on the point. Matter, it is said, is extended or quantitative substance. It has dimension. It consists of parts, and so it can be dissolved. Spirit has no parts, no dimensions, no quantity, no extension. It has only qualities.

I do not think that any better definitions have ever yet been given. Body is quantitative, and can dissolve into its parts. Mind is not quantitative (they say) and so cannot dissolve into parts, or die. So said the learned Aristotle, and we cannot go much further. Modern definitions of "matter" do not improve on his. It is generally said to be "that which occupies space," which is the same. Spirit is like a mathematical point. It has no magnitude.

It may not sound so warm and thrilling to say that your soul is a nonquantitative substance, but on this point depends entirely your hope of immortality. You have to prove that your mind is immaterial or unextended. What are the proofs?

The Roman Catholic philosophy, which prides itself on being the severest and most logical, while it is merely the most medieval, is very confident about the matter. I have ideas of things: pictures of them in my mind. Let us say that I have a mental picture of a beautiful woman; that I see one before me. I am conscious of the picture as a whole. I may fasten my attention on her hands, her feet, or her bosom, but I may also contemplate her as a whole. Now if consciousness is a function of the brain, how can I see such a picture as a whole? Each cell in the brain is composed of innumerable atoms, and each atom is composed of tens or hundreds of protons and electrons at an appreciable distance from each other. Each atom, nay, each electron, ought to have its own fraction of the brain-picture, on the materialist hypothesis. The unifying principle at the back of matter must, surely, be a spiritual substance, a soul, which has no atoms or parts.

This seems to me a better argument than most of those one finds in modern or modernist literature, but the fact only shows how feeble the modern arguments are, for even this one is a tissue of fallacies.

Take a sleepwalker. He has no consciousness. On the spiritual hypothesis, his soul is switched off from his body. One theory of sleep is that the cells of the brain draw in the little branchlets or fibrils by means of which they ordinarily communicate with each other. Something like that happens in the brain. In any case, the soul, the supposed seat of consciousness, is switched off for the time being. The body acts mechanically and automatically. Yet objects are "seen" as a whole, as the conduct of the somnambulist shows. He avoids every obstacle. Put a table in his path, and he goes around it.

The truth is that those who use this and similar arguments are simply building on the temporary ignorance of science, just as they do when they try to prove the existence of god. Candidly, we do not know how we see objects as a whole. For the matter of that, we do not know how we see them all. That is precisely why many philosophers deny the existence of material objects. There are, they say, early images in the mind, and from these you may more or less riskily infer that there are objects corresponding to them outside the mind.

The whole mental world is still obscure in the last degree. Psychology is largely a matter of verbiage, and it declines entirely to speculate on the nature of mind or consciousness. I have read all the attempts to explain consciousness, and I cannot see anything in them but words. The human brain is immeasurably the most complicated structure in the universe (as far as our knowledge goes). It consists of hundreds of millions of cells put together in a structure which we as yet very imperfectly understand. Each cell consists of millions of molecules, put together in a way we do not understand at all; for molecular structure is below the range of our most powerful microscopes. Each molecule, further, consists of atoms, put together in a structure which we very imperfectly conjecture. And, finally, we now know that each atom is a wonderfully complicated world of protons and electrons.

So who is going to say what the brain can or cannot do? Men who use the argument I have described imagine a brain-image of an object as a miniature picture of it spread over a certain surface. It is not in the very least likely. What would the brain-stores of a very learned man be like in that case?

Or take it this way. You see a tree. Some sort of image of it is impressed on your retina by the waves of light. This is no more a picture of it than a phonograph record is a tune. Then this impression on the retina is converted into some kind of movement along your optic nerve. It is now still less like a picture of the tree. The nerve-movement is converted into something else in the optic center of the brain, and finally you see a tree. To say that there is a little picture of a green tree with yellow oranges in your brain is absurd.

We do not know what the machinery of perception is and cannot build any argument on it. We do not know where and how we are conscious of the objects we see. We have not the least idea what it is that is "stored in memory." We have still less idea how we can fuse together all the particular men we ever saw and get the general abstract idea of "man." We do not know how we can draw inferences and make arguments. We know very, very little about mind.

Then, you say, it may be a spirit. If people were content to say "may be," we should not much object, though we have seen strong reason for thinking that it is not. What we object to is the religious assertion that it *is* a spirit. There is no proof of this whatever. For all we know, it may be merely a function of the brain.

And a hundred things suggest that it is merely a function of the brain. Mind varies with every minute alteration of the brain. A fever or an opiate speeds up the mental activity. A heavy meal or a dose of alcohol benumbs it. During the [First World] War the Germans gave their shock troops a certain drug which made them giants in "spirit" for the time being. It is difficult to understand—impossible, in fact,—how a spirit-mind can act on the brain; but it is the easiest thing in the world for chemicals to act on the mind. We shall see more of this in the next chapter.

To sum up the whole matter, people generally *assume* that the mind is a spirit and the reason generally is that mind is "so very different" from matter. I quite understand the force of the impression. At times I reflect on this wonderful thing, that this whole vast universe can be mirrored in the tiny mind of man; that the mind can reconstruct scenes in the story of the earth which passed away millions of years ago or scenes in the interior of atoms which no eye will ever behold.

But it is only the imagination that is impressed. The intellect waits upon the advance of science. Not in our time— not, possibly, for centuries—will science unravel the mysteries of mind and brain. Mind *ought* to be far more wonderful than anything else in the universe. Its organ, the brain, is the most wonderfully intricate material structure that exists. When we understand that structure, we shall know whether or not consciousness is merely a function of it. Until then there is no logic whatever in pretending to say what can, and what cannot, be a function of the brain. There is no force in saying that something *must* be a spirit until you know positively that it *cannot* be material.

4

What Is Personality?

Until not many years ago the provision of milk in a mother's breast just when she needed it for the babe was a mystery. But for the delicacy of the subject I suppose that preachers would have chosen it as an impressive proof of the soul or god, and their audiences of women would have been deeply impressed.

Then a London professor set about investigating the mystery, and it is a mystery no longer. A woman's breasts are stimulated by a certain chemical. This chemical is poured into the blood by the fetus in her womb, and, naturally, the more the fetus grows, the more of the drug it produces, so the stimulation reaches its maximum at a time when the fetus is largest and is ready for birth. We can extract the chemical from the fetus of a rat and inject it into the veins of a rat which is not pregnant, and, though she does not require milk, she gets it.

You might take that as a parable. What science cannot explain today it may explain tomorrow, and the man who builds on its ignorance today will retreat tomorrow. For the last hundred years the theologian has been engaged in retreating: of course, "upon positions which were prepared in advance."

But I quote this to introduce a new aspect of the question of immortality. What on earth can the rat or the fetus have to do with it? Nothing whatever, but this material secretion which stimulates the milk glands introduces us to new discoveries in science that do bear on the subject.

If you open a physiological book of the last century, you find many references to the telegraphic system in the human body. The nerves are the wires. The brain is the central station. A fly hits against your eye. A message goes to your brain: an order is flashed back along another nerve: and in a fraction of a second you raise your hand and brush the fly away.

The new discovery is that there is a postal, as well as a telegraphic, system in the body. Letters are posted in the blood, and they travel round the vascular system until they reach their destination. In other words, certain small glands in the interior of the body pour chemicals in the blood, and these are carried round and round until they reach the part which they are to stimulate. I will assume that every reader has heard of the thyroid gland, which is one of them, and I must refrain here from any further account.

The point is that the thyroid and some of the other glands have a most profound effect upon our mental vitality and our personality. The character of an old man can be rejuvenated. A born idiot can be transformed into a sane child. Whole districts in which a large portion of the children have for ages been born idiots (cretins) have been rid of idiots by means of thyroid extract. When we have mastered the chemical nature of the stuff produced and poured into the blood by these glands, when we can make it in the laboratory and sell it in the drug store, it will be time to talk of the musician playing on the piano. For then the chemist will play on the "spirit," on human nature, as no religion ever did.

Now the point of this is that we have one more illustration of the way in which mind depends upon body. We were, of course, quite familiar with this. In the very early days of science temperaments or characters were divided into four main types: the lymphatic (sluggish), choleric, bilious, and sanguineous. This was crude psychology, but it expressed the well-known fact that a very great deal of a man's personality depends upon his bodily qualities. Nerve and brain, stomach and liver and pancreas, blood and muscular tone, all have their respective influences on what we call character. Drugs still further complicate the character. I spoke once of the "genius" of a certain British author to a man who is the highest living authority on him. "Genius?" he said: "No, simply nicotine." A man drunk is often not the same man sober. And now we know that the quality of a man's endocrinal glands has an even greater influence on those qualities which make up what we call his personality.

The question therefore naturally arises: What sort of a thing will the soul be even if we suppose it to be immortal? Philosophers, as I said, assume that the mind is a spirit. It is singular how little they think of proving this. The order of ideas and that of material realities seem to them to differ so profoundly that the former is referred to a spirit-world; when, as we saw, we do not know sufficient about the brain to say that ideas *cannot* be aspects or functions of material things. However, philosophers rarely believe in personal immortality. Psychologists still more rarely accept it. There are very few real experts on the subject in the world who do.

Now you know why. It was always quite impossible to imagine how the mind could think without a brain. As usual, it was cheerfully said to be a mystery—while the general public imagines that the soul "explains" thought. Now we see that whether the soul could or could not think when it is disembodied, it certainly cannot have anything like the personality it had on earth.

Think of every little trait or feature of the child or the woman you love. The golden curls or fine glossy hair, the soft blue or fine brown eyes, the round limbs and graceful carriage— these things, of course, go down into the grave forever. But even the features of character depend entirely on the body. The vitality, the sweetness or quaintness of disposition, the warm affection, the reserve or the spontaneous effusiveness—all depend on bodily organs. What will this disembodied soul of wife or mother, whom you hope to meet again, be like? What will even memory be without the brain? For whatever be its nature, it depends vitally on the brain.

This doctrine of immortality begins to look very far from simple and satisfactory when you examine it. The pagan Romans, whose cold and vague attitude toward a future life was so much derided by the new Christians, were nearer the truth; quite apart from the fact that the view of the future life which Christianity brought was, with its eternal torment for the majority of the race, the most repulsive yet formulated. The Roman, like the Babylonian, believed that the soul survived the grave, but it was a pale, thin "shade" that survived. He had little interest in it.

In psychology, in fact, the idea of soul has long since been surrendered. It became the science of the mind, not of the soul. But the more progress the science made, the less it liked the idea of a substantial something of which ideas and emotions were individual acts. All that we are sure about now is that there are ideas and emotions and volitions. The world of consciousness is a world of atoms of consciousness. But whence comes the unity of the conscious life? It may, surely, come from the unity of the nervous system, the most completely centralized structure in the universe.

In other words, we find once more what we find in *The Futility of Belief in God* (Little Blue Book No. 1060): religious ideas not only melt into mysteries and unintelligibilities when you analyze them, but they are decidedly in conflict with our new knowledge. And it is not a question of evolution only. The science of psychology itself must have a deadly effect on belief when hardly one in ten of our psychologists believes in personal immortality. But the most deadly solvent of religious belief—let the anti-evolutionists realize this—is the patient examination of the so-called evidence which is offered us in support of it. This makes ten agnostics for every one that is made by the teaching of science.

I have said that materialism seems to me too dogmatic an attitude. It might be added that what we commonly call matter is now known to be *not* the ultimate reality of the universe, so it may be questioned if the term is a good one. Matter is composed of mysterious things which we call electrons and protons. Many physicists say that it is composed of "energy," and some call themselves energists. It seems more likely that ether is the ultimate reality, and those who like labels might adopt that of etherist. Most of us prefer to leave it to a much wiser generation to put a comprehensive label on the universe.

Yet, as I said in connection with the existence of God, the agnostic attitude must not be understood to mean that it is a quite open question whether the mind is or is not a spirit. I mean, we must not in the least suppose that the chances are even. The thinkers of the race have been weighing this question every since the days of Socrates. In fact, we can clearly enough see that educated men, apart from the clergy, were speculating on these fundamental religious issues in Egypt four or five thousand years ago. In Asia, as we may find in *The Human Origin of Morals* (Little Blue Book No. 1061), Buddha and Confucius came to the conclusion that religious speculation was a waste of time several centuries before the great thinkers of Athens appeared, and the earliest Greek thinkers seem to have been of the same opinion.

Now, what has been the general issue of these thousands of years of thinking about god and the soul? Has anything been settled on the religious side? Nothing. We are no wiser than the first thinkers. We rule out the "proofs" of immortality given by Plato and St. Augustine, and we have no better to offer. In the spiritual scale of the balance there are only arguments about which there is no agreement whatever.

The whole weight of our new knowledge falls into the material scale, against immortality. Modern philosophy, when it started, at once shattered the older proofs, which Roman Catholics still use. Evolution proved a deadly weight against the belief. Psychology, as it evolved, turned against it. Physiology, as this chapter shows, throws all its weight into the materialist scale. Not a single fact has been discovered in the last hundred years that favors the view that the mind is a spirit. We remain open-minded, but with little doubt about the result.

5

Modern Theories of Immortality

Ours is the age of reconstruction, not only of all beliefs, but of all arguments for the beliefs. We think of man as profoundly conservative in his nature and anxious, if possible, to cling to his old beliefs in some form. And this is said to be particularly true of religious beliefs. Many imagine the soul of the race in our time as heroically braving the great new waves of thought in an effort to preserve its religious identity.

All this kind of rhetoric is false to the obvious facts of life. It is always a few who do the reconstructing of beliefs and arguments, and these few are nearly always people who have an interest in the survival of the beliefs. This is, surely, a plain reading of the facts of life. The majority of the race is profoundly indifferent to the disappearance of old traditions. New religions, even of the most liberal character, make little appeal to them. Even the movement for Ethical Culture, which describes itself as religion without the least theology, makes almost no progress either in America or in England.

And the interested or professional few who fight for the old ideas are chiefly successful when they use the unsound old arguments. We see much of this in *The Futility of Belief in God,* and we shall see more of it throughout the whole series, and there is a remarkable instance of it in connection with the immortality or spirituality of the soul.

It is the very common practice of telling our age that it is becoming, or is in danger of becoming, materialistic. This is screeched from a thousand pulpits and is even echoed in the columns of the press. Just let us consider it for a moment.

What is materialism? We treat it fully in another volume, and for our present purpose merely take it to be a disbelief in spirit, either divine or human. In that sense our age is certainly becoming materialistic. But why the note of horror and alarm in announcing the fact? Here is the fallacy of the argument. There are two meanings of the word materialism. One is the proper and natural meaning: the belief that all reality is material or quantitative. That is merely a mental theory.

But we also use the word to mean *the absence of ideals,* and, though this has no real connection with the preceding meaning, the two are deliberately confused. The world is told that ideals are lost unless we cling to the belief in spirit: as if it mattered two cents to a man's conduct whether his mind was quantitative or nonquantitative! As to social or collective idealism, one would surely expect that, when the hope of heaven dies, men will develop more and more their idealism of a better earth.

The whole of this familiar rhetoric is confusion of thought. Materialists do not deny the existence and importance of mind and its ideals. They deny that these are spiritual. But because the world has been accustomed to regard the mind and its ideals as spiritual, the cry is raised that "spiritual realities" are in danger, when the question is merely whether they are spiritual or not. A great man of science like my friend the late Professor Loeb would smile at the idea that his interest in science ought to diminish when he came to the conclusion that the mind is only a function of the brain. Most of us ought to smile at the idea that we will turn the world upside down because we have come to the conclusion that it is the only world we shall ever know!

But I give a reasoned and constructive view of life on rationalist principles in another volume. Many people genuinely believe that no such philosophy is possible. We shall see that it is easy. Meantime, let the believer reflect that he does not understand this only because he has never yet had occasion to make such a philosophy for himself; and, above all, that the world *is* getting steadily better while faith decays.

Let us finish with the "proofs" which modern theologians attempt to give of the immortality of the soul. The more learned of them frankly give it up. Immortality is, they say, a matter of faith. An infinite god can make us immortal, and the Bible says that he will.

This, unfortunately, is to prop up a feeble and tottering belief by means of two other beliefs which are just as feeble and tottering. We see this about the belief in god. We may see it about the belief in the inspiration of the Bible. I cannot imagine what comfort the argument gives to anybody.

Other religious writers prefer to say that, while they cannot prove the spirituality and immortality of the soul, they can suggest reasons for believing in it. For instance, some of them say, science has discovered that the conservation of energy is a law of the universe. No energy is ever destroyed or annihilated. So the mental energy must persist. The soul must survive.

An extraordinarily feeble argument. Let us admit—with certain reserves about the energy of electrons—the general truth that energy is never annihilated. But it is just as universal a law that energy is constantly changing its form, and, when the energy is associated with a complex material structure, and that structure breaks up, it is bound to change its form very materially.

Luther Burbank recently startled California, of which he was one of the greatest citizens, by declaring that he does not believe in the immortality of the soul. It disappears at death, he said, just like the life of the old automobile that is condemned to the scrapheap. That is a very good figure of speech. The life or soul—the particular function—of the automobile does not continue to exist. It breaks up into the separate energies of the parts of the machine or of the fuel which is no longer used. So says the materialist of the human mind, and what he says is perfectly consistent with the law of the conservation of energy. The law is not that any particular form of energy shall be preserved or conserved *as such.* It is rather the reverse.

Sir Oliver Lodge, who uses this argument, helps it out with another which is worse. I am constantly asked why a "great physicist" like Sir Oliver Lodge is found on the side of religion. Well, to begin with, he is not a "great" physicist, and, secondly, his science, physics, is precisely the one which least qualifies him to deal with religious questions. It has nothing to do with the nature of life or mind. But, thirdly, I have shown in my *Religion of Sir Oliver Lodge* that there is not a single doctrine of the Christian religion which he accepts, and, fourthly, he is just one of the survivors of the little scientific group which was duped by mediums in the early uncritical days of spiritualism.

Sir Oliver has discovered a remarkable principle which helps him to prove the immortality of the soul. Whatever really exists just goes on existing: always existed and always will. The mind really exists, therefore. . . .

Quite simple, isn't it? In fact, rather too simple. There is no such principle. Matter and energy go on existing *in some form.* That is all we can say. So the body goes on existing in some form, but its functions do not. The whole argument assumes what it sets out to prove: that the mind is not a function of the brain.

Then there is a philosophical argument which has of late years gone the round of "advanced" religious literature. It is called the argument from the conservation of values. A man grows up to wisdom and settled character and personality. Can we suppose that all this is to be thrown away by the act of death? What a shocking waste it would be if each individual is to learn laboriously, to become wise and to form his character, and then it were all to be annihilated: if the human race were during millions of years to construct its wonderful science and art and idealism and all were to end in the great silence of the death of the race.

So the argument runs: and the answer requires little reflection. What does the great inanimate universe care about waste? What does it know of values and of conserving them? Quite clearly, the argument has no sense whatever unless you mean that you are appealing to god. It is not very forcible even then, but it has not the least meaning except insofar as it relies on the wisdom or power of god, and we have seen how far you can appeal to that.

Other writers keep recalling from its well-merited rest an argument which was much used in the early days of science. The matter of the human body is always changing. Nerve and muscle wear out. Even the material of the bones is withdrawn and replaced in the course of time. It is commonly said that the entire material of the body changes every seven years. We do not, in fact, know how long it takes. We can put hands on a pigeon's leg bones, and see how long it takes for them to disappear, but no man can say the time for all the organs of the body, especially the brain. There is, however, no doubt about the fact. Probably I have not now a single atom of the body I had ten years ago. Yet I am the same person, and I vividly remember experiences of ten, and even forty, years ago.

Quite so. But I have already explained that mind is said to be a function of the brain, and, if so, it depends upon the structure of the brain, which does not change. Molecule by molecule the material is renewed, but the structure even of each individual cell remains unaltered. An idea, we saw, is not a miniature picture of an object, spread over a certain area. It is an activity of the brain.

Suppose you regard the beauty or grace or symmetry of an ancient cathedral as a function or aspect of its structure. You may go on for centuries restoring a beam here or a few stones there. It is conceivable that in time you might renew nearly the whole material of it. But the identity remains.

It is conceivable that—if it were worthwhile—you could in time renew all the parts of your automobile. There might not be left a single bit of the original machine. But its function would be unaltered, and most particularly if, as in the case of the human body, there were some subtle way of replacing atom by atom, without disturbing the structure, the original material of the machine.

Finally, there are those who find an argument in the moral order. Insofar as this argument merely appeals to the fact that man has moral perceptions, a criticism which I make in *The Futility of Belief in God* (Little Blue Book No. 1060) disposes of it.

Moral law is social law, and it is as easily formulated by the mind itself as what we commonly call law is. Philosophers like the famous Kant or the modern German thinker Eucken* write about conscience and the moral law as if they had never taken the trouble to study men in the flesh. There is no such thing as a "categorical imperative," as Kant said. There is no such thing as an eternal moral order existing apart from the material order, existing before humanity was born and independent of it, as Eucken says. For most of us there is just a moral ideal implanted in us by education and evolved out of the needs of social life.

Nor is there any force whatever in the claim that this commanding law implies that god is prepared to reward the observer of it in another life. You cannot rely on the disputed existence of god to prove a disputed immortality. But there is another way of ramming the argument, and this requires longer discussion.

---

*Rudolf Christoph Eucken (1846–1926). (Ed.)

6

The Freedom of the Will

In several of his works my friend Professor Haeckel, whose fine and vigorously honorable character was personally known to me—I discuss the myth of his "forgeries" in another booklet—gives God, Freedom, and Immortality as the three fundamental religious beliefs. And it is unfortunate for the believer that the independent experts on these subjects are overwhelmingly against him. Few philosophers believe in a personal god. Few psychologists believe in free will or personal immortality.

I can imagine a religious reader saying to himself that in this case at least he does not care a rap about the experts. He will quite understand that I am nowhere trying to intimidate him with the authority of experts. I merely ask him to reflect on the significance of the fact that all or the majority of the men who have devoted their lives to a particular study are against him, and that on his side are only a few preachers with poor training and little knowledge.

But what he will reply here is that the best expert on himself is himself. He knows whether or not he has free will, he says. When it comes to a question of his summer holiday, he is free to choose between ten different places. He pleases himself whether he wears a straw or a felt hat, whether he is a Republican or a Democrat, whether he reads any more of these Little Blue Books or not.

And if a man has this pure power of choice between alternatives, his mind is not of the order of material realities. There is no freedom for matter. It goes where it is pushed or pulled. Even the moth which flies round the candle is ruled by a purely mechanical principle, which we have traced. If man is free, if his will can act without compulsion or coercion from any power or motive, then man *does* stand out from all the rest of the universe, and the law of death may not be for him. His mind must be an indissoluble spirit.

But plain folk must recollect that psychologists have just the same consciousness as they have, and have a far greater ability to analyze it. They have been analyzing and disputing about this apparent consciousness of freedom for a century. And they are now generally agreed that it is an illusion. Surely that has some significance.

Let us take it in our own way. When you say that you are free to choose—say, between the train and the surface car,* or between the movies and the theater—you are using rather ambiguous language. All common speech for expressing mental experiences is loose and ambiguous. You have the two alternatives —movies or theater—in your mind. You hover between them. You do not feel any compulsion to choose one or the other. Then you deliberately say to yourself—not realizing that you have thereby proved the spirituality of the soul, which has made apologists perspire for centuries—"I choose Norma Talmadge."

Well, let us examine it patiently. In the ordinary acts of life you behave automatically. You don your clothes and shave and eat and walk, and even work, in a mechanical way. The motive arises, by routine, at the proper moment, and the action follows. It is only in grave things—such as whether you shall go to see Norma Talmadge or Bebe Daniels†—that you use

---

*A streetcar, as distinguished from an elevated train. (Ed.)

†Norma Talmadge and Bebe Daniels were two popular film stars of the day. (Ed.)

your freedom. To be quite accurate—am I not right?—it is only when two or more motives seem to have about equal force that you are conscious of your freedom. If one motive, if the reason for doing one action, is palpably stronger than the reason for doing the alternative, you do not hesitate. The "will" follows or acts on the stronger motive.

Why, you ask, do I put "will" in inverted commas? It may shock you to know that psychologists are not sure that there is such a thing. You may be surprised to know that your "will" is only a theory (like evolution). What you are really conscious of is a series of acts. It is just a theory of yours that there is a thing you call your will behind them.

Well, to come back to the "acts of will." When you hesitate between two courses, do you for a moment doubt that your will eventually follows the one which seems to you wiser or more profitable? Yes, I know. Just to prove your freedom you may choose the less wise course. But in that case you merely have a new motive thrown into the scale. Your "will" always follows the weightier motive. How, then, is it free? All that you are conscious of is the hesitation of your mind, because for a time one motive balances the other. They may remain so balanced that you do nothing, or leave it to others to decide. But if you do decide, you are merely conscious that the battle of motives is over and the stronger carries your will.

But, you ask, what about moral responsibility? What about praising and blaming people for their conduct? What about crime and its punishment? Is not our whole social and moral system based upon the theory that a man is responsible for his actions?

Again we have a tangle of rhetoric, which we must unravel, and some serious questions which we must seriously discuss.

The reader who is genuinely alarmed about crime and criminals, either on account of sermons he has heard or from his own reflections on the subject, ought to study the statistics of crime. In such matters it is the facts that count. He will find that crime has steadily decreased during the whole modern period when free will and religion have been just as steadily abandoned. The great reformers in the treatment of crime, the men who have done more than any others in initiating measures which led to its reduction—Beccaria,* Bentham,† Lombroso‡—were rationalists who did not believe in free will. It is a century and a half since their ideas began to be adopted, and in proportion as they were adopted, crime has diminished.

In the United States crime is abnormally high. But this is no reflection on the normal character of the American, which is finer than it ever was before, and is as fine as any in the world. The very large figures of crime are due to political corruption behind the Parole Boards. In England and other normal civilizations, where there is at least an equal amount of unbelief, crime has been reduced by fifty percent and it is now at its lowest level.

So much for the pulpit cry that we are in danger of an orgy of crime and violence. I give the figures in another booklet. But, you will say, we cannot logically blame the criminal if he has no free will.

What does it matter? The practical point is that you can make unsocial conduct or crime very unattractive to the man who may be disposed to indulge in it. The sentence inflicted today is not so much a punishment. It is not the revenge of society for an injury done to it. The penal system is now an intimidation. We lodge in the mind of the possible criminal a very strong motive to deter him.

The cat which steals your chop or your chicken has no free will. You admit that. Well, do you take it in your arms and say: "Poor dear, you only acted according to your nature?" And are you logical if, on the contrary, you thrash it, to teach it propriety? When you pat on the head the dog or the horse that has done good service, and so encourage it to repeat its performance, are you acting foolishly? You know better. Good feeling as a reward of good conduct is a new motive to the will. The frown or the stroke of society is a deterrent.

---

*Cesare Beccaria (1738–1794). Italian economist and jurist, who wrote the first systematic treatment of rational criminal punishment. (Ed.)

†Jeremy Bentham (1748–1832). English jurist and philosopher. (Ed.)

‡Cesare Lombroso (1836–1909). Italian physician and criminologist. (Ed.)

So far it is easy. Determinism, or the theory that denies free will, has no social consequences whatever, except good ones. When we grasp the real nature of the criminal, we treat him more wisely. We are, on determinist principles, slowly eliminating him.

Candidly, it is not so easy to talk about praise and blame and responsibility in other than criminal matters. When you have a social practice founded upon thousands of years of wrong ideas the readjustment is not easy.

It is clear that we can still imprison or otherwise annoy people who act criminally. But it is really on a question of reading a new shade of meaning into the words [that] . . . we do not "punish" them in the old sense. It is just as clear that a man is responsible to his fellows for any evil consequences of his acts, and, since the moral law is social law, he has moral responsibility. I mean that society has just as much right to protect itself from breaches of those laws which we call moral— such real moral laws as truthfulness and justice—as it has against breaches of common law, and for this purpose it can quite sensibly use the sytems of reward and punishment which we call praise and blame. We praise or blame the act, because of its consequences. We know quite well that there was no free will in it.

Did you ever applaud Tetrazzini* or some great actor or actress? Did you ever cheer an athlete? There was no free will in the performance. A singer happens to have an exceptionally good larynx; an athlete to have some abnormal muscle or nerve. But what would you say if a man in black rose in the audience and said: "Don't applaud. These people are not responsible for their gifts."

Well, tell that to the next man in black who says that we cannot on determinist principles praise or blame conduct. Until good or social conduct is automatic, as it will be one day, society has every right to smile encouragement or frown its dispproval. The price of a lie shall be an unpleasant quarter of an hour.

---

*Luisa Tetrazzini (1871–1940). Famed Italian opera singer. (Ed.)

As long as we have something of the nature of the cat left in us, we may be treated as even a humane person treats a cat.

7

Paradise Lost

The only great epic which the Christian creed ever inspired was *Paradise Lost*. Childish as many of the details of it seem to us today, there is a human element in the legend which inspired Milton to write his finest work. What are the losses of thrones, of fortunes, of wives in comparison with the loss described in the story of Eden? Yet how many ever shed a tear over it? And now that we are losing, not merely a legendary Eden, but a whole eternity of perfectly happy existence, how many shed tears today?

To some future historian this modern age of ours, the age of transition to real civilization, will seem extraordinarily interesting, most particularly in regard to the loss of religious beliefs. We surrender without a sigh the age-long belief in an omnipotent father and in an endless life where pain and labor are unknown. Nay, we are gayer than the world ever was before: so merry that the pessimist tells us that our thoughtless and universal gaiety, our dancing and attending shows, our unprecedented development of games and sport, will surely lead to catastrophe. And the merriment is greatest just in those centers of population, our large cities, where the belief in god and immortality is fading most rapidly. Surely, even the preacher will not deny that? It is one of his favorite themes.

I leave it to this historian of the future to analyze this strange situation. One of the most capable of the French historians has recently written that one reason why the French people turned so easily against the Church at the Revolution, and are in the enormous majority quite indifferent to it today, is that they were never really Christian. They remained pagan at heart, he says. The new creed was observed, not profoundly believed. Perhaps most of us have remained pagan at heart.

But, although these questions of history and the statistics of crime and morality must be separated for adequate treatment in other Little Blue Books, I must here and there summarize, in general terms.

The preacher cannot have it both ways. If we are the most pleasure-loving generation that the earth has known since Roman days—you will find, as usual, that he knows nothing about Roman days—it is no use telling us that the loss of belief in god and immortality is a terrible and saddening experience. It is no use saying that we must exclude from our schools whatever leads to infidelity so that our children may guard "the priceless treasure of their faith." Apparently they will be happier when they have lost it.

I doubt if anyone in the world has a larger experience with "unbelievers" than I have. Three times I have lectured all over Australia and New Zealand, and three times in the United States, meeting rationalists everywhere. They shower letters upon me from all parts of the world. I meet them in International Rationalist Congresses. And I have never met man or woman, out of the thousands who tell me that my books and lectures have influenced them, who did not say, "Thank you."

An archdeacon of the Church of England, a zealot of the grimmest type, once tried to persuade me to cease writing on religion on the ground that it "robbed" people of their faith. I truthfully assured him that, to judge by their letters, one might as well talk of "robbing" them of dyspepsia or gout. He at once changed his tone and said that "this idea of happiness is a pagan idea." And when I courtesouly reminded him that it was he who introduced it, he lost his temper, as saints sometimes do, and the next day he walked out of a surface car the moment I entered it.

I fear that, except the last incident, it is typical of the clergy. The world is saddened by the clouding of its faith, and the world is made with gaiety and games. The Christian religion is just revealing the full force of its divine message, and the world is returning to paganism. There is a revival of religion, or at least no serious decline of it, and the world is sinking into an abyss of depravity. Rationalism is a gospel of despair, and rationalists are the very gayest people of this gay age.

As part of the penalty of being one of the leading militant rationalists, I have been reading these desperate and incoherent statements for thirty years. Have patience with me if at times my pen does not seem to have been dipped in the milk of human kindness. Are the clergy sincere? Or do people fool them? Do they fool each other?

Facts are the best diet. I am writing this in the smoking room of an ocean liner. It is noon on Easter Sunday (1926). Divine service is just over. We have a clergyman aboard. Two nights ago (Holy Thursday Night) I saw him reading his breviary (I looked over his shoulder) or book of prayers in this crowded smoking room, and a youth interrupted him to ask if he would have a liqueur. The book closed with a bang, and, turning his back with a laugh on the Almighty, he accepted the cognac. People much admire him for these things. He has had quite a good congregation this morning, especially of ladies whose spirituality is, during the rest of the week, not obtruded. And now they are back in the smoking room, and the ladies who ten minutes ago were, with sweet expressions, saying "Hallelujah" because the Lord has risen, now noisily demand cigarettes and cocktails, and rattle the dice box and glance with disdain at the dour wicked atheist at the writing table, and wonder what he is writing.

Certainly not a sad world, whatever else it is. But these are the believers, you may say. More or less, perhaps: but one-third of them are making this voyage for their health because the doctor gave a hint that the gates of heaven were getting visible in the distance. In church they sing, angelically:

"I long to be where Jesus is."

And they move heaven and earth to put off the evil day as long as possible. Do they really believe in immortality? Even American psychology could not analyze their minds.

For those of us who *think,* the surrender of the old beliefs means no pain and no hypocrisy. Conduct, the world's character and morals, we do, as I said, discuss elsewhere. Let us examine the beliefs first. The main question is whether they are true or not. They are useless if they are not true.

But there is one emotional aspect of the matter which must be considered here. In that famous last speech which he prepared, but did not deliver, Mr. Bryan said that "Christ had made of death a starlit track from the grave to eternity," and, of course, modern science had blotted out the stars and left the dying without any hope or consolation. A very pretty sentence, almost equal to the historic cross of gold. I will not stay to ask whether the light of the stars was in Mr. Bryan's eyes when he realized that. . . . Well, *de mortuis nil nisi bonum,** which means that it is only the dead atheist that you may decry.

But, seriously, how many believers in immortality have you known whose eyes shone when the death sentence was pronounced or when the dread moment came? I have seen both rationalists and Christians die, and I have buried scores of both. There was no starlight in the eyes of the believers. Perhaps it is a tinge of rationalist prejudice that colors my recollection, but I seem to remember very plainly that there was more serenity in the eyes of the unbelievers. More than one rationalist whom I have known, quietly put his affairs in order and ended his life. I intend to do the same myself, instead of waiting for grumpy old age and its maladies, when my vitality slackens, and the human comedy begins to bore me, and none will be hurt by my departure.

We are masters of life and death, we rationalists. It has been a fine adventure, this half century of conscious existence,

---

*"About the dead [say] nothing but good." (Ed.)

with all its labor and trouble and injustice. Huxley* once sincerely replied to Kingsley, who sympathized with him on the death of a child, that they were proud and happy to have had the child just those few years with them. That is the spirit. An hour of sunlight is better than none. To have been born and lived and died is, for the man who knows how to live, a privilege and an opportunity that he might never had had. You have clasped the warm hands of friends. Perhaps you have had the good fortune to love and be loved. You have had the joy of seeing your children slowly rise through the phases of blossoming and ripening around you. You have known the fragrance of wine and flowers, the delights of art, the fascination of science, the joy of battle in a good cause. . . . How can any man have the effrontery to grumble that the feast is not eternal?

I write, not rhetorically, but simply what I think and feel; what people who have given up religious beliefs generally think and feel. Those of us who have had decades of more or less successful life say quite sincerely with old Walter Savage Landor, when he bade good-bye to his friends:

> I have warmed my hands at the fire of life.
> It sinks and I am ready to depart.

And it is not fanciful to think that the last man to linger on this globe will say the same to the dying sun. As I have explained in another book, this earth is likely to be habitable for another two hundred million years. We do not know such things positively. One of those great catastrophies that do often occur in the universe might melt our solar system into stardust long before that time. But as the system has avoided accidents for one or two million years, we may feel fairly confident about its stability.

In that case, we have reason to think, this globe will support human life for a further two hundred million years. The sun

---

*Thomas Henry Huxley (1825–1895). English biologist and freethinker. (Ed.)

will grow cooler, rosier in the heavens. The cold will enwrap the globe. Ice will creep from the poles until it mantles the entire globe. But ages before that time the chemists of the future will have made the race independent of agriculture, and the engineers of the future will do marvelous things to defeat the cold. In the end the cold must conquer, and mankind must close its tenancy of this planet.

It will not grumble. The "happy accident" of the habitability of this globe will be a matter for congratulation. The race will have had a good time by two hundred million years from now. As we are at last, now that we have done with revelations and otherworldliness, really advancing in wisdom, I assume that within a century or two life will be worth living for everybody: no poverty, no crime, no violence, no stupidity, very little disease, and a long life for the majority. Accidents will occur less often, and, though I do not believe that man will become less emotional—that he will sacrifice one of the richest elements of life and pleasure—the emotion will be more healthily adjusted to reason. Two hundred million years of this kind of life will be considered a fair allowance.

Long before that time we of the prehistoric age will have been forgotten. Possibly scholars will keep in their chronicle just this fact about our age: that it was the time when men ceased to believe in god and began to believe more in their own powers; ceased to believe in heaven and so began to make earth more tolerable. They will probably say that it was a good thing for the race that the myth of immortality was exploded and the dream of paradise lost in a discovery of the earth.

Lies of Religious Literature

1

What Is a Liar?

Gregory VIII, the great Hildebrand, was one of the most deeply religious of the popes. He believed as literally and unwaveringly in a living Christ and a future reward in heaven as one believes in the existence of the sun at broad noonday. Mighty and absorbing as was his pontifical ambition, he was one of the few popes who made a serious, if infelicitous, effort to remedy the gross moral corruption of his Church. He was an incarnation of religious and puritanical fanaticism. But when, in one of his letters, he had occasion to comment on the virtue of truthfulness, he weakly observed that "even a lie that is told for a good purpose, in the cause of peace, is not wholly free from blame" (*Epp.,* IX, 2). The inference was obvious. If a lie in the cause of peace was almost wholly free from blame, a lie in the sacred cause of religion could hardly have the shadow of a stain on it; and Gregory so used lies and forgeries not infrequently.

It is a far cry from popes of the eleventh century to Christian scholars of the twentieth. The papal fabric is in ruins, and men smile at the antique pretensions and draperies of the modern pope who is enthroned amidst the ruin. Revolution has succeeded reformation. New ideals shine in the minds of men. Has the Christian estimate of truthfulness changed? We have revalued the code of conduct which made abject servility the virtue of

109

the mass of men and permitted oriental pomp and arrogance to lords of Church and State: which ignored a worldwide cruelty and made a virtue of self-torture: which laid a bond upon the intellect and a malediction on the few fair things that would gladden the heart. We have made new virtues of honor, manliness, social justice, service, self-consciousness, and self-appreciation. The preacher promises us a better earth, not a surer heaven. Has he changed his ideas about lying for the right?

I begin with Christian scholars because they are higher representatives of modern Christianity than popes or bishops or preachers, and because in another Little Blue Book (*The Forgery of the Old Testament,* No. 1066)* the reader has seen an example of their work which must have intrigued him. These scholars, for instance, unanimously admit that the man who wrote the book of *Daniel,* in the first person, lived several centuries after the events which he pretends to have witnessed. But no scholar will admit that he was a liar or a forger. These scholars all admit that *Deuteronomy* was not an ancient law romantically found in the Temple, but a contemporary document written by the priests who falsely declared to King Hilkiah that it *was* an ancient book accidentally found by them. But no Christian scholar will agree even with the great prophet Jeremiah (VIII, 8) that it was a "lie." Nearly all these scholars hold that the Old Testament, as we have it, was put together by priests who in their own interest completely altered old documents and filled in the narrative with fictitious details, about the year 500 B.C. But we are to call them "redactors," not liars and forgers.

It is admitted by most of these scholars that a number of the Epistles of Paul, written in the first person, were not written by him, and that whoever wrote the Gospels, and put on them "according to Matthew," etc., was not relating what contemporaries of Jesus said. It is admitted by all scholars that thousands of the lives of saints and martyrs are spurious, and that the medieval power of the popes was based upon a massive foundation of spurious decrees, letters, and other documents.

---

*In this volume. (Ed.)

But for a blush of moral indignation you will search in vain this literature of modern Christian scholarship. No work which uses the word "lie" is deemed worthy of their notice. Few of them dare raise the question whether these things ought or ought not to be called lies; and the few who do, invariably say that they are not lies, because the aim of the writer was pious.

And if this is the quite general attitude of Christian scholars, we know what to expect from the writers and preachers who are not scholars. Right here, however, let us be clear that we must make a very large allowance for ignorance. I had come years ago to spend a fortnight in close association with a dozen clerics, nearly all of some distinction in the Church of England. A canon, at the close, insisted on having my impression, and he at length forced me to say that my chief impression was of their "colossal ignorance": ignorance of science, history, philosophy, and sociology. He sadly acquiesced. Their periodical literature, popular books, and published sermons, all over the world, will inform any man of that.

So the great mass of the quite untrue statements that are made by clerics week by week are not lies. They dogmatize on the gravest questions of life, history, and philosophy; and they are ludicrously unequipped even to hold a timid opinion on such matters. The literature they read is rubbish. How far they are responsibile for their ignorance, how far they evade knowledge because it might prevent them from making the statements they do, is another matter. But they rarely say what they know to be false. Some unquestionably do. Within the last few weeks a man has told me that he compelled a preacher to admit, after a sermon, that, for edification, he had deliberately made a false statement. Preachers, however, merely reproduce the statements of their current literature, and it is with this that I concern myself.

Now it has been one of my chief and most deliberate aims throughout this series of Little Blue Books to show that religious literature is full of false statements. Societies for the propaganda of skepticism are generally feeble and unsystematic. There is little pedagogy, and less psychology, in their procedure. They are too apt to entertain skeptics with their literature, because it is upon the bank-balances of skeptics that they depend. It is one of the most massive testimonies to the soundness of the skeptical position that, though the vast organizations of the churches are opposed only by one or two societies of such dimensions as to be entirely negligible, there has been so tremendous a decay of belief. An organized educational effort, based upon a careful psychology of the believer, would soon detach further millions from the churches.

And one of the chief counsels which would arise from this scientific study of the situation is that the first step is to convince the religious man that his literature deceives him. Very naturally he believes that the writers of his sect are competent and honest. It is amusing to meet one of these people and hear his polite and hesitating confession that the attitude of the unbeliever entirely bewilders him. He has read only religious work, and these invariably misrepresent skeptics and falsify the evidence in their own favor. That "the people wish to be deceived" may or may not have been true in the Middle Ages, when the proverb arose, but it is not true today. In certain emotional circumstances one does, of course, find that attitude. During the European War I found no editor in England wiling to publish an article of mine, thought I was not a pacifist, proving that current statements about crime in Germany were false. Indeed, on another occasion, when I proved that the so-called military experts underrated Germany's strength by three million men, one educated lady after another declined to listen to me, protesting that she did not want her optimism undermined. I have earlier quoted Henry James admitting immortality because he "liked to think it"; and I have at the moment before me a letter from another well-known writer who surprised the world by suddenly admitting it, after years of public denial of it, yet says to me: "It is a matter of feeling and desire."

In a career like mine one meets scores of such instances, yet the attitude is exceptional. Ninety-nine men and women at least out of every hundred resent deception and would reconsider any beliefs which had been formed on, or were protected by, untruthful literature. I have, therefore, through my whole series of Little Blue Books, on the one hand given explicit references to the original authorities for any statement which was likely to be seriously questioned, and on the other I have persistently pointed out that religious literature is habitually and pervasively false. The first aim of any rationalist should be to convince the reader of this. When the boast is made that there are still several hundred million Christians, your religious neighbor will at once grant, on reflection, that the gross total matters nothing. What consolation can be derived from the faith of 250,000,000 grossly ignorant Russian, Balkan, and Spanish-American peasants, or from the 150,000,000 other peasants and poorer workers of the higher Christian countries? The only "issue" for any serious man is what proportion of believers remain amongst properly educated peoples amongst whom critical literature circulates.

We shall try to determine this in another Little Blue Book, but, however many tens of millions of educated believers there may be, the significance even of this is very gravely reduced if you can show that their belief is based upon or buttressed by mendacious literature. This I have shown abundantly, but the point is of itself so important that I propose to devote one Little Blue Book to a condensed and convincing summary of the evidence. Apologetic literature is monstrously untruthful. I am not sure if I have not in some other book quoted the following passage, but it will bear repetition. On August 20, 1903, one of the leading British religious weeklies, the *Christian World,* had an editorial on "Candor in the Pulpit," and it said:

> A foremost modern theologian, by no means of the radical school, has recorded his significant judgment that one of the main characteristics of apologetic literature is its lack of honesty; and no one who has studied theology can doubt that it has suffered more than any other science from equivocal phraseology.

Even in his rare moment of candor, you notice, the Christian editor has to describe as "equivocal phraseology" what his more

learned (but anonymous) colleague bluntly terms dishonest language. It is notorious. For decades Catholic writers have accused
Protestants of lying, and their Christian brethren have not been
slow to return the epithet. Fundamentalists have accused modernists, and have been accused by them. They cannot, therefore,
affect a tone of indignant surprise if I take them at their respective
estimates. Their whole case for the faith, agaisnt skepticism, is
based upon untruth. It will be convenient to devote two general
chapters to the systematic falsification of history and science
and then give as many as possible concrete instances of falseness
from current religious literature.

But falseness, let me repeat, is not lying, and I must justify
the title of this book. Take a few specific false statements;
Haeckel's forgeries, Paine's or Voltaire's deathbed agony, and
so on. They have been proved over and over again to be false,
but preachers and writers still use them, and may believe them.
But the man who started those statements lied as plainly as
Mrs. Eddy* did when she claimed originality or Mme. Blavatsky†
when she claimed a revelation. I have shown that literally thousands of statements in religious literature are lies in this sense.
The modern writer, innocently or otherwise, repeats lies, not
simply inaccurate statements. The lives of most of the martyrs,
for instance, are lies pure and simple. The accounts of the Roman
persecutions of Christians are for the most part putrid lies. We
need not make a psychological investigation in the case of each
modern writer who repeats them, or try to determine his degree
of culpability in not checking them by available literature. The
Christian case is based upon historical lies. This is my thesis.

My Little Blue Book No. 1243, *The Failure of Christian
Missions,* discloses another aspect. The head of a mission sends
home the number of his "native Christians." He includes all
who once professed belief (perhaps to get free education) and
does not count out seceders. Are those lies? The effect is a gross

---

*Mary Baker Eddy (1821–1910). Founder of the Christian Science Church.
(Ed.)

†Helena Petrovna Blavatsky (1831–1891). American theosophist. (Ed.)

deception. Similarly writers speak of 350,000,000 Christians in Europe (where there are not more than 200,000,000 people, nearly half Russian and Balkan peasants, who ever attend church), of the grave increase of crime (which is decreasing everywhere except in certain special American conditions), and so on. Are those lies?

Let us say that they are objectively lies. The task would be endless if we wanted to determine responsibility in each case. I have repeatedly known apologists continue to make statements which were of value to them after they so plainly learned the truth that they cannot any longer have believed implicitly in their statements. But, as I said, the lies are generally repeated in ignorance. The statements themselves are nevertheless lies, and they would be characterized as such if they were personally libelous and so came into court. That a person carelessly or innocently repeated lies would not persuade the court to speak of them as "inaccuracies." We will follow the juridical model. Religious literature is full of statements which are lies; and we may at least add that the truth is, in modern times, easily accessible to the writers who repeat those lies.

2

The Falsification of History

The simple believer who fancies that the raging controversies of the world need not disturb him, that he can dispense with evidences and criticisms of evidence, does not reflect that religion is essentially a collection of statements. What he is apt to regard as preeminently his religious life, his emotional life, necessarily follows upon beliefs; and beliefs are statements of acts based on some kind of evidence. In its broadest and simplest sense religion makes the extremely controverted statements that man's mind is of so peculiar a nature that it can and will function without a brain—that it is spiritual and immortal—and that the universe somewhere bears certain marks or imprints which must have been made by a supernatural, eternal, spiritual, and at least extraordinarily powerful being.

But religion is almost always embodied in a larger creed, and each of the chief creeds is based upon an extensive series of historical statements. We are concerned here only with the Christian. And to take this again first in its simplest form, moderate modernism or Congregationalism—Unitarianism, when it *is* Christian, makes much the same historical statements —and taking only, for the moment, its essential statements, it affirms that there was a being named Jesus Christ in Judea about nineteen centuries ago; that in power, personality, and teaching he was

116

quite unique; that he founded a church which Europe was persuaded to accept, and that this Church has, by means of his teaching, proved of enormous moral and social value to the world, and has lifted civilization far above the moral level of pre-Christian civilizations.

That is the essential series of statements, but, naturally, there are right and left wings even here. We may say that any man who calls himself a Christian affirms—this is the minimum—that Jesus Christ existed, that his teaching was unique and supreme, and that we have that teaching in the gospels. Those of the right wing, the majority, and with them the members of all other Christian sects, affirm, in addition to these things, that the Jewish ethic was already superior to all others; that the Jewish books are "inspired"; that Christ exerted a supernatural power over natural laws and was therefore God; that he was executed, but his body came to life again; and that the gospels are authentic records of these things.

Then you have the great body of the less educated Protestants and all the Catholics, who make further series of historical statements; that the human race began with a definite and highly gifted pair whose posterity degenerated; that the black race is inferior because it was cursed, and that there was a terrible destruction of the living world by a deluge; that certain gifted Hebrews performed miracles and predicted long-distant events; that the Jews were the first to worship one God and cherish the modern standard of conduct; that Jesus was miraculously conceived by a virgin and was superlatively removed from the moralists in his person and teaching; that ten terrible persecutions were launched against the early Church and tens of thousands were picturesquely tortured and martyred; that the world at last voluntarily adopted the new faith and rose in moral character, and so on.

Well, let us make no bones about it. Every one of these statements is an historical untruth. I am, for the moment, not taking particular historical statements of Christian writers, but the essential affirmations of the man who calls himself a Christian. The simplest case is that of the man who, though he may not even believe in a personal God or personal immortality, calls himself, for prudential reasons, a Christian. Now it is not a lie to say that Jesus really existed. I think it probable that he did. But do not leap to the conclusion that a lie is, therefore, merely what I do not happen to believe. The difference is that my opinion—and it only runs to probability—is based upon a general interpretation of a large number of events in the first and second centuries; but the opinion of the man who so far admires Christ as to call himself a Christian is plainly based upon the Gospels. And I say very emphatically that lies about these gospels pervade the whole of our religious literature and are the real bases of the belief. The proper experts on these documents—practically all of them Christian ministers —have come to certain conclusions about them, and the statements which are commonly made about their conclusions are mendacious.

I am not accusing these divines of lying and am certainly not so lacking in humor and manner as to call every conclusion that does not favor skepticism "a lie." That may seem superfluous, but thirty years' experience of this controversy make me quite aware that it is not superfluous. So let us be quite clear. The lie is to represent that the biblical experts have "vindicated the gospels" or traced their appearance to within a reasonable distance of the death of Christ. That is a lie, and a basic lie.

As I have shown in Little Blue Book No. 1084 (*Did Jesus Ever Live?*)* the theological experts are agreed that they have traced *some* gospel, not any of our existing gospels, to between twenty and thirty years after the death of Christ. It seems to me that the evidence even for this is feeble, though scholars are entitled to their opinions, but to represent this as a vindication of the trustworthiness of *our* gospels is a lie. It does not matter what rationalists say here. The point is that the theological experts agree, as a majority, only that some slender ac-

---

*In Joseph McCabe, *The Myth of the Resurrection and Other Essays* (Buffalo, N.Y.: Prometheus Books, 1993), pp. 67–115. (Ed.)

count of the words and actions of Christ existed twenty-five or thirty years after his death. What was in it that they do not know, but they, again as a majority, agree that what a Christian regards as the most fundamental parts of the existing gospels were *not* in it; and, in any case, the ordinary rules of history and common sense compel us to look with distrust on an oriental narrative that cannot be traced within twenty years of the date of its hero.

Some excitement has been caused in the religious world recently by the fact that the late Georg Brandes adopted the opinion that Jesus never existed. Brandes was, in point of fact, a master of modern literature, but not a man particularly equipped for discussing questions of ancient history. He may or may not have been right, but religious periodicals are not only wrong in their criticisms of him, but untruthful. One that lies—in both senses—before me says airily that Brandes has just learned of a fantastic theory which was annihilated by Bishop Lightfoot in the middle of the nineteenth century. That is the tone of these religious periodicals. The aim is to apply an opiate to their readers, so that they will neither read Brandes nor reflect on the real difficulties of that position. It is untruthful.

Another recent illustration I find in one of the most substantial books written on the religious side in the last few years. This is *Progress in Religion to the Christian Era* (1922), by T. R. Glover, written for the Students Christian Movement. Glover is a fine scholar and an honorable man. It must not be thought that I am introducing him as a specimen of the clerical liar. He is, in fact, not a cleric—which may explain a little—but a serious and exceptionally conscientious writer on pre-Christian religions. Most of these he appraises with a candor which will certainly be useful to the Christian students. It is not the kind of thing they usually read about "paganism." But I quote the book because in one section it comes perilously near the customary practice of buttressing the Christian position with untruthful statements. This is the section on the religion and morality of the Jewish prophets, which are represented as higher than any then known in the rest of the world and not to be explained by the enviroment of the Jews. This is not a section of religious history on which Mr. Glover has any particular authority, and one may complain very severely of his repetition of conventional Christian statements which will not bear close examination.

As we have seen, the whole story of the evolution of ethics and religion has been, and is, quite falsely represented in Christian literature. The lies about ancient Babylon are repeated all over the world today, although it is twenty or thirty years since archeologists discovered the truth about the Babylonians and historians showed that the statements of the Greek historian Herodotus are false. The legend that the Hebrews were the first to hold monotheism is another quite universal lie of religious literature, for Egytpologists had traced it at an earlier date in Egypt half a century ago, and orientalists are familiar with it in Persia. The legend that Christianity introduced the sense of sin and repentance is just as untruthful and just as universal. Nearly every religious writer continues to describe the progress of religion and morality in the past as if archeology had taught us nothing, and as if the ideas of the Persians, Pythagoreans, Platonists, Stoics, etc., were quite unknown to us.

My main point is, however, that the simplest, most common, and most confident of all Christian statements—that we know from the gospels that Jesus taught a unique and sublime morality—is based upon untruths. Whatever we think of the question of the historicity of Jesus, it is one of the most difficult things in the world to extract any reliable information about him from the only biographical documents we have; and, even if we take the teaching ascribed to Jesus in the gospels as authentic, although, as I have shown, this would be a drastic violation of all ordinary rules of history, that teaching is not unique in any single particular or in its entirety. As I have said in another Little Blue Book, I know of only one occasion on which any historical committee sat down to examine the gospel on ordinary historical principles, and all its members were Christians. Yet they candidly admitted that no single saying of Jesus in the Gospels can be proved to have existed in the first century.

Yet this "uniqueness and sublimity" of the teaching of Jesus is seized upon by all Christians, and by many who are not Christians, as the one really indisputable thing. It is convenient. One escapes the attentions of the dervishes by proclaiming that one really is a Christian: explaining, in private, that the virgin birth is folly and the resurrection a piece of silly gossip—that what one means is the wonderful ethic of Jesus. There is, in fact, a type of rationalist who prides himself on the superiority of temperament he displays by joining in this ethical eulogy of the Bible and Jesus. Only last year the British Rationalist Press Association issued a work entitled *Light on the Bible.* "Light" is usually understood to refer to youth, yet the aim of the book is to foster an admiration of the Bible on the ground that the truth or untruth of its statement does not matter. The writer, Mr. F. J. Gould, knows his subject well, but is of the ethical school that boasts of being purely constructive and "inspirational." The result is that he speaks of "the good scribes" of Ezra's school without any intimation of the way in which they forged whole books in the interest of their caste and he leaves the mind of the reader a complete blur as to what is true or false. He takes the Pharisees as they are falsely caricatured in the gospels, and, in an admiring chapter on the parables of Jesus, says not a word about the hundreds of parables of the Talmud, some of which are plainly copied in the Gospels, and goes off to Buddha for a parallel. And those of us who do not consent to this kind of education of the public are described as having "no sense of history"!

The Christian creed in every form, even the kind of new Christianity which professes to have no creed at all, is based upon a falsification of history. The character of the peoples, religions, and moralities before the Christian Era is always, and generally grossly, misrepresented. I need quote no instances. Every single popular book and article that refers to them misrepresents them. Then the universal assumption which is the basis of all this fulsome talk about Jesus and his teaching—the notion that biblical scholars have won any sort of historical credibility for the Gospels—is totally untrue. Next the history of the world *after* Christ is just as grossly perverted. The extent and nature of the growth of Christianity are falsely stated, the character and sufferings of the early Christians are mendaciously represented, the fine qualities of the Romans are miserably slandered, the utter viciousness of the mass of the Christians after Constantine is concealed, the triumph of Christianity is described as spiritual and not a word said about the score of imperial decrees which forced it upon the Romans, and the subsequent lapse into barbarism is concealed under vague and untruthful generalities or spurious lives of saints.

This tradition of lying is carried over the whole Christian Era. I have exposed it in twenty Little Blue Books which are of themselves more than enough to justify my title. There is hardly a single aspect of the history of the last nineteen centuries as to which Christian literature is not radically untruthful. Protestant literature, it is true, is willing to depict the Middle Ages in dark colors, but the Protestant writer is invariably untruthful about the early Church, the post-Reformation period, and modern times. It is a veritable orgy of historical lies. This book would not suffice to contain a mere summary of the historical untruths I have exposed in some twenty or thirty books of this series.

3

Misrepresentation of Science

If you put this situation to an educated Christian, he will probably admit with regret that my strictures are generally justified. He will make a serious exception only in regard to what I have called the principal untruth; the assumption that the gospels are so far credible that we can confidently speak of Jesus as a very great or unique moralist. You will invariably find, on close scrutiny, that this is precisely the point on which he has read least. Not one man in ten thousand has ever studied the highly technical and often strained arguments by which biblical experts affect to trace some sort of gospel to about the year 60, and then attempt to give it some sort of credibility. However, the general historical untruthfulness will be admitted, and the defense will be that Christian scholars perceive it, but it is a delicate and necessarily very slow task to reform popular Christian literature.

I do not admit even this. In my other Little Blue Books on the various sections of history I have quoted entirely false statements from recent Christian writers who have the greatest authority in their sects. But, instead of returning to these, I will illustrate my point by passing on to science and showing at once that, quite apart from the really gross misrepresentations of Catholics and fundamentalists, which we will take separately, the highest actual authorities on the subject are gravely culpable.

The present acute controversy about evolution has inspired a fairly large literature. Curisiouly, there was otherwise a slump in religious books during the last few years. I look over the voluminous list of works published in America and England and I find in 1925 and 1926 a material diminution of those works of piety and edification which once formed so large a part of the year's crop. The question of religion and science has, however, again been thrust forward, and a score of writers has proved once more that there is no conflict. With most of these I deal in Little Blue Book No. 1211, with others I shall deal in later chapters, but one or two may best be considered here.

Religious Certainty in an Age of Science (1924), by Professor C. A. Dinsmore (of Yale), is a title that promises much, but it is disappointing. There is much religious certainty in the book, but very little science. The statements are vague and we need not linger over them. As far as they go, they support my thesis. A professor of theology at Yale ought to know better than to speak about "the Supreme Power which science recognizes." Professor Millikan is not science. When such a statement is supported by quotations from Tyndall, who was so pronounced an agnostic that he was always in his day classed as a materialist, we are surprised. It is, moreover, not in the least true that evolution shows "an increasing purpose running through the ages." Even a man who recognized purpose in evolution does not see any "increase" in it, and science knows nothing about such a purpose. What it teaches about evolution is so unfavorable to purposes that most evolutionists are agnostics. On the other hand, the story of the evolution of man, which, as I said, has a very drastic relation to the dogma of man's spirituality and immortality, is merely said in this book to "open great spaces for faith in immortality." Yes, but the spaces happen to be empty.

Another work by a distinguished theologian to which I turn with my customary eagerness and docility is Professor Shailer Mathews' *Contributions of Science to Religion* (1924). Let me repeat my warning that I am here making a collection of lies as well as liars. A lie may be repeated in ignorance and innocence, and Dr. Mathews is a highly respectable man. But this book of his is funny. It is a large book, and five-sixths of it consists of an admirable series of chapters on science by competent professors. These thirteen essays are good summaries of scientific teaching, but the authors never say a word about religion! The title of the book, in other words, is monstrously inaccurate. However, when the scientists have done, Dr. Mathews adds four chapters on religion. The funny thing is that *he* has really little to say about science, but there are just a few pages which must be considered.

In the whole four-hundred-page book I find only two definite relevant points. The first is that the new physics has made an end of materialism. I have dealt with that already ancient superstition in another book. It is rubbish. As I showed (in Little Blue Book No. 1229), the materialistic scientists of the nineteenth century precisely expected and hoped for just such a development of our conception of matter as has occurred. It was—really, men like Dr. Mathews ought to know this—precisely the Christian men of science (Stewart, Tait, etc.) who did not want it. There were seventy or eighty known species of atoms. Were they created or evolved? A moment's reflection should tell anybody that the materialists held that they were evolved and the theists that they were created. As to the realities of which we now find "matter" is compacted—it remains matter just the same—protons, electrons, and ether occupy space just as well as iron does. The position of the materialist is untouched.

The only other definite point in the book is that the "new astronomy" also favors religion. How? Why, we learn that it shows that "the ultimate activity is infinite." This is worse than ever. Every materialist was always convinced that reality is infinite whereas astronomers, and most of us, generally, say nowadays that it is quite impossible to prove that anything is infinite. In fine, "ultimate activity" is a phrase which astronomers would not recognize. We understand, of course. It is the voice of Millikan; but he is not "the new astronomy."

Fresh to hand comes a new work by the leading expert on these matters, Professor H. J. Osborn, *Evolution in Religion and Education* (1926). I fear that Professor Osborn, who once wrote some fine scientific works, has become a mere book-maker. It is the same old stuff as in *The Earth Speaks to Bryan,* but the price is larger. However, Professor Osborn has in the meantime, one supposes, seen some criticisms of his peculiar views, and this must be his mature and final word. One hopes, at least, for his credit, that it is final.

One of Osborn's greatest mistakes was to adopt an old—twenty years old—theory of that archsophist Oliver Lodge to the effect that men of science were largely materialistic in the nineteenth century, but are now converted. I have repeatedly shown this is a lie, and I open the new book—of which it is one of the chief theses—to see what serious evidence Professor Osborn now offers us. It is dismal.

For the United States he gives us the famous manifesto of thirty-five "prominent Americans" who declare that they believe in God. If Osborn happens to have any friend with a sense of humor—I doubt it—he ought to submit his manuscripts to him. As proof that there has been a change, a return to spirituality, in American science he tells us that he and Millikan managed to induce fifteen scientific men (including themselves) out of several hundred to say that they believe in God! It is really funny. Fifty years ago you could have got four or eight times that number. And it is interesting, in view of what Dr. Mathews says of the "new astronomy," that there is only one astronomer in the list; and, I may add, only one psychologist.

Well, well, you say, perhaps this religious revival in the scientific world is in Europe. Try Germany. All that Osborn offers in the way of witnesses are Rudolph Eucken (who "initiated the rapprochement of science and theology") and W. Rathenau. But Eucken is merely a dreamy metaphysician who knows little more about science than Ed Wynn* does, and Rathenau is merely a business man. Try England. We get Canon Barnes, an anonymous writer in *Nature,* Lloyd Morgan and Professor J. S. Haldane. I need only remark that Haldane was saying the same things in 1888 and Lloyd Morgan not much later. Instead of

---

*Ed Wynn (1886–1966) was a popular comedian of the day. (Ed.)

their indicating a "return swing of the pendulum," as Osborn says, they are just survivors of the old theistic group, and even they are not Christians. Could anything be more unfortunate and more unscientific? The public is assured by a distinguished man of science, a man of large and long acquaintance both in the American and European scientific world, that there has been a notable change of attitude toward religion on the part of scientific men; and as evidence of this, for England, he gives the names of two out of a hundred men of science, and they are merely survivors of the last generation and for the rest of Europe not a single scientific name.

Almost equally grave exception could be taken to a large number of passages in Osborn's latest book, which is sure to be used as a sort of bible by the modernists. "Rationalists," he says, "are more humble now because in the hunting fields of human thought the scientists have taken as many falls as the theologians" (p. 56). That is an incredible misstatement, a scandalous encouragement of the fundamentalists who bleat that science is "always changing." And "Rationalists more humble now"! I ought to know something about them.

Professor Osborn is not even consistent. Who these dogmatic materialists of the last century were he never tells us. I suspect that he would name Haeckel;* and Haeckel was not only a materialist, but he opens his *Riddle* with the too humble statement that the "attainment of truth" is an "immeasurably distant goal." Osborn has got there in a stride and puts the humility on us. But, as I said, he is not consistent. He does say a good deal about one famous rationalist of the last century, Huxley, and he actually gives the reader the impression that Huxley was religious. Huxley's views on religion were, he says, "diametrically opposed to Herbert Spencer." Not exactly: Spencer was too religious for Huxley. Professor Osborn can only quote the fact that Huxley favored the use of the Bible in the school. On this he quotes a passage to which, completely forgetting for once

---

*Ernst Haeckel (1834–1919). German scientist and philosopher, author of *The Riddle of the Universe* (1899). (Ed.)

his scientific method, he gives no reference. Had he done so, the reader might have learned the date of it. Huxley changed his mind about the Bible in the school long before he died.

Even in strict matters of science Professor Osborn gravely misleads. To please or disarm fundamentalists he reiterates that "the ape is *no longer* in the line of human descent." Professor Elliott Smith, a higher authority, says precisely the opposite, and the personal dogmatism of Professor Osborn is deceptive. As I have explained in another book, no existing ape is, *or ever was,* in the line of human descent, but if we found the bones of man's ancestor of the Oligocene Period we should pretty certainly call them the bones of an ape.

And the fact that Professor Osborn does these things in the interest of religion becomes quite apparent when we find him repeating his earlier language about Cro-Magnon man: a race which appeared in Europe toward the close of the Ice Age. There is not another archeologist or anthropologist in the world who would admit that, if we could trace this race to its place of origin, we should find it rising suddenly and mysteriously above its fellows. Yet that is the "new science" which Professor Osborn is offering to believers. He grotesquely exaggerates Cro-Magnon man, and he then suggests that his appearance means an "emergent evolution"—of souls, of course. I know only one man of science (religious, of course) who agrees with him, and he is not an authority on the subject; yet Osborn puts this before his readers in book after book as if it were the accepted teaching of science instead of being merely his own eccentric and accommodating opinion.

These are the three best books of the last two years, when all America has been talking about religion and science; and all three are written by professors. After this you know what to expect from the Baptist preachers, the Sunday School teachers, the zealous old ladies, the medical men with a turn for piety, the journalists, stenographers, and soft-drink manufacturers who turn out most of the stuff from which the mass of religious believers learn all that they know about science. Heaven forbid that I should accuse these simple souls of lying! In order to lie you must know the truth, and my impression after reading a great deal of this literature is that the writers would not turn a hair if you told them that Arcturus was a Silurian starfish, the Archaeopteryx a Brazilian beetle, and the epididymis a Mexican orchid. We shall see a little about their weird ideas in later chapters. They are generally concerned about evolution.

I invite the reader to note, in conclusion, that science is *less important* in connection with religion than history is. Science has, as I have shown in another book, a real and serious bearing on the questions of the existence of God and, especially, of the immortality of the soul. In this respect, apart from the evolution of man, its teaching is not so much falsified as ignored. But history has to be falsified from beginning to end by Christian writers. Every single historical point I have treated in this series— the character of the ancient civilizations, the story of the Hebrews, the person and teaching of Christ, the establishment of Christianity, every phase of its history, and its relation to art, science, tolerance, philanthropy, morals, civilizations, etc.—is obscured by a mass of untruths in all Christian literature. Christianity, as such, is based essentially on historical untruths. A quite truthful and full account of man's development, as now agreed upon by all our historians and archeologists, would put an end to its pretensions. It remains to see how this untruthfulness is distributed amongst the various sections of the Christian World.

4

Fundamentalist Fudge

I have space only to consider three types of religious literature: the fundamentalist, the Catholic, and the modernist. Since the fundamentalist and the Catholic are closely allied in their defense of medieval doctrines which the educated world has discarded, it might seem better to take them together and for a third type choose the intermediate class, the large body of believers who are more liberal than the fundamentalists and less liberal than the modernists. But both Catholics and fundamentalists would regard it as an outrage to be coupled together, and I have the tenderest regard for their feelings. Both believe in eternal torment, a blood-atonement, and so on. Both boast that they surrender not a tithe of ancient Christian doctrine at the bidding of modern culture. Yet there is a material difference. Catholic literature is generally written by men with a far more complete and lengthy education, and it is therefore far more dishonest. We will take it separately.

Not dishonesty, but ignorance, is the outstanding characteristic of fundamentalist literature. I began this series of works with the aim of writing so temperately and courteously that even a fundamentalist or a Catholic could read me throughout. If any have had the courage to continue to do so, they must pardon the degeneration of my manners. The title of this book gives them the reason for it. In covering once more the familiar ground, but in a more rapid and complete survey than I have ever made before, I have been so shocked and moved by the falseness of the Christian literature I consulted that it seemed hypocritical to use other than stern or derisive language. The contents of my books have, surely, justified this. These things are lies, and the fact that a particular writer repeats them innocently does not disarm criticism. No writer who ventures to instruct the public on these matters is justified in such innocence and ignorance today.

The outsider is often puzzled by the situation. Does not the fundamentalist, he asks, perceive that he has no learned men on his side, and that Christians in proportion to their education lean to the modernist or semimodernist position? No, he does not. He has a pathetic belief in the learning of his own orators and writers. How is he to know? I have debated in California with a local modernist leader who assured his followers that he had made a thorough and academic study of geology. I knew better, and I gasped when the man claimed that he had found a human boot embedded in (not thrust into a crevice of) Triassic rocks (which are about 250,000,000 years old). But my audience believed their pastor, that he was a competent geologist, and so accepted his conclusion that the rocks were only a few thousand years old and that the boot pointed to the Deluge.

It is especially the opposition to evolution which has spread a thick layer of the fundamentalist fudge over America, and it is almost enough to examine it in this connection. When I undertook a series of lectures and debates on the subject in America in 1925-1926 I studied a large collection of anti-evolutionist literature. The statements in them are so bewildering that it was difficult to credit the writers with sufficient ignorance to think them honest.

There was an *Evolution at the Bar* (1922), by a Philip Mauro, who seems to have been a lay evangelist. He made such statements as (p. 56, and the italics are his) that "the Engis skull is supposed to be *the oldest known up to now.*" What would a fundamentalist say if he found a rationalist writer remarking that Herod was an ancient Jew in the days of Abraham? It is a just parallel. Virchow is described as "one of the very greatest of chemists"; which is about as true as if one described Mr. Edgar Guest as a Jesuit priest. Huxley is said to have "definitely rejected the Darwinian theory" late in life; and for this we get a quotation which belongs to 1870 (twenty-five years before Huxley died) and is falsified. Haeckel, the arch-evolutionist, is made to say that "most modern authorities" are opposed to it; which refers to the earliest days of the controversy.

On this point, and it is of very great importance, I found Mauro and the fundamentalist writers generally positively dishonest. When I came to address fundamentalist audiences, I discovered, as I had anticipated, that they were quite ordinary decent folk with plenty of common sense. If all the scientific authorities in the world were agreed that evolution was a fact, these men and women had too good a sense of proportion to think that they could smile at the agreement. It was therefore a vital and invariable trick of their literature to represent to them that the scientific men are not agreed, but that great names in science can still be quoted against evolution.

This is done in four ways, and each is sheer mendacity. Scientific men who did oppose evolution in the nineteenth century, but died at least twenty or thirty years ago, are quoted, and no date is given: for instance Sir J. W. Dawson (died 1899), Saporta (died 1895), Virchow (died 1902), Sir R. Owen (died 1892), and even Professor Pfaff (died 1886). The second trick is to turn all sorts of men who did or do oppose evolution into "professors of science": for instance Professor Dennert (a philosopher), "Professor" Wright (a geological clergyman, not a professor), "Dr." Etheridge (or *Mr.* Etheridge, a Museum assistant, died 1903). Dr. R. Watts (a preacher of years ago who knew nothing whatever about science), George T. Curtis (a lawyer, whose "recent book," as Mauro calls, it was published in 1887), "Professor" Townsend (a clergyman who died ages ago and knew nothing about science), "Professor" Gerard (a British Jesuit unknown in science), etc. The third trick is to name men like Professor Bateson, who reject Darwin's particular theory of evolution, but are thorough evolutionists. The fourth trick is to name scientific men who opposed materialism, not evolution: Lord Kelvin, Professor Dana, Professor Beale, etc.

There is actually not one university professor of, or authority on, either botany, zoology, anatomy, physiology, biology, biochemistry, psychology, anthropology, or prehistoric archeology in America, Britain, France, or Germany who does not claim that evolution is true. There has been no such person for twenty years. And when I made that point, and challenged my opponents to name one, I saw a new light in the eyes of my fundamentalist hearers. The whole of their literature has lied on that point. Their Mauros and Townsends and Fairhursts, and all the rest of them, utterly deceive their readers. Catholic writers like McCann and Father Gerard and Zahm are, as we shall see, just as untruthful.

Professor George McCready Price* is the nearest approach to a geologist in the movement. He teaches in a Seventh-day Adventist College in Nebraska and has not an atom of prestige in science; and he has taught geology (after various other subjects) only for a few years. He believes in the Flood and denies the Ice Age: which would bring upon any real geologist a commission of medical men to investigate his mental health. He dupes his readers by telling them that there is a "new geology," not explaining that he means that he personally is at war with all the geologists in the world. His fantastic views are based mainly on certain strata in the lower Rockies which I have personally seen; and his interpretation of them is perfectly ludicrous. There is nothing abnormal about them.

This anti-evolution drivel is fairly typical of the kind of statements of fundamentalist writers. Another group of them try to show that *Genesis* is quite in accord with science, and they give weird and fantastic versions of "what science says."

---

*For the debate between Joseph McCabe and George McCready Price on evolution, see *Debates on the Meaning of Life, Evolution, and Spiritualism* (Buffalo, N.Y.: Prometheus Books, 1993), pp. 91–140. (Ed.)

Usually their writers and speakers are content to give them heavily caricatured scraps of "science" and play for ridicule. I have heard one of their leaders entertain a crowd for ten minutes with his account of the "wild guesses" of scientists at the central heat of the earth, and I found he was quite unaware that it was a simple and necessary deduction from the increasing temperature of the rocks as we go down. Others I have found ridiculing science on account of its pretension to measure the size and velocity of waves of light; and they were amazed to hear that these things were settled nearly a century ago and have stood every possible test since then.

Even more serious is the reason why these good people listen willingly to misrepresenation and abuse of science. The "Word of God" tells them what to belief about the origin and early history of things. This means that they add further piles of untruths to the historical untruths which I have described as common to all Christians.

If you can once convince a fundamentalist reader that his literature is totally wrong, whether it be innocent or no, invite him next to say why he believes the Old Testament to be the word of God. He requires no education to perceive that the fact that the writers of it say so is no evidence. He knows his Bible well enough to know that Christ never said so, hence there is no need to discuss the authority of Christ. He does not believe in infallible popes, so he has no authority to impose the belief on him. You will find in the end that he has taken the word of the priests who forged *Deuteronomy* and the priests of the Ezra school who later forged other books and falsified the whole. And when you point out that nearly all the early stories of *Genesis* are found in Babylonian literature in so closely parallel a form that a "revelation to Moses" is out of the question, that we have found the Babylonian code of laws and see how the "Mosaic code" borrowed from it, that Egyptian stories and hymns also are turned into Hebrew in the Old Testament, that our knowledge of Persia and Babylon is now so good that we find some of the Old Testament writers ludicrously ignorant of things which they profess to have witnessed, and so on, you will find the usual situation. On all these points his literature is grossly untruthful.

There is needed in America a specific movement for the instruction of what are called fundamentalists. They despise the professors who profess to show to them that science is quite in harmony with religion. Over and over again they have told me that they have more respect for skeptics. They despise modernists, as men who profess to regard the Bible as "the Word of God" and take very human liberties with it. They are a formidable and earnest body, a phenomenon of American life which few take the trouble to explain. Great Britain, for instance, imports nine-tenths of its foodstuffs, and its population is, therefore, in an enormously greater proportion an industrial population living in or near towns, which are never far apart. Only a few thousand live in England in the condition of intellectual isolation in which millions of farmers live in the United States. As a natural result they have a vast body of poorly paid and abominably educated ministers, and a literature circulates amongst them which an informed person finds it difficult to read. It would be a mighty gain to America if these people could, without passing through the intermediate stage of modernism or semi-modernism, be induced to adopt a sane human idealism on human affairs, and it is a grave and dangerous error to set them aside as negligible.

5

Catholic Truth

The chief difference between the fundamentalist and the Catholic from my present point of view is, as I said, that the average fundamentalist minister has had a very scanty education, but every Catholic priest has had at least a prolonged education. Two or three years of language (chiefly Latin) and history, two years at philosophy, and three or more years at theology and bibical study may be regarded as the standard education of a priest. It is rarely less than seven years, and it usually lasts from thirteen or fourteen to twenty-four years of age. I should add that most of the time is wasted in learning things which scholars would regard with disdain. The average priest has not even a good knowledge of Latin, his history is a ridiculously false version of the history of the Church, his philosophy has scarcely any relation to what is known as philosophy in a unviersity, and of science he has hardly any knowledge whatever. Even the Jesuit, who artfully maintains the popular fiction that his education is remarkably efficient, is a badly educated man.

Hence with the average Catholic preacher I have no quarrel. He has had no real training in the branches of culture which a man ought to master if he would dogmatize on the great problems of life. It is, in fact, amazing to see millions of men and women hanging upon the lips of preachers, who are no more fitted than themselves to discuss serious matters. Some day the world will rub its eyes and, with a laugh, advise its preachers to try auctioneering or someting useful. Priests are quite capable of believing, though probably half of them do not believe, what they preach.

Catholic journalists are even less qualified, and thus the greater part of the information which reaches the average Catholic comes to him from men too ignorant to know what is true and what is false. The average believer rarely reads books written by scholars, even of his own sect. The weekly sermon and religious periodical are his oracles. It is a providential arrangement, for these are just the sources of information which can most innocently convey the most outrageous untruths to him.

The Catholic journalist is, in fact, as a rule less scrupulous than the priest. Lay writers are not much favored in the Catholic Church, and they seem to betray their consciousness of this in the zeal of their statement. Father Zahm, one of the chief Catholic writers on science in America, and Dr. Walsh, medical professor in a Catholic college, are, as I show in another Little Blue Book (No. 1142), as far removed as possible from delicacy and accuracy in their statements, but quite the worst specimen I have ever encountered is a work (*God or Gorilla*) by a Catholic layman, Alfred W. McCann.

The author, in discussing the supposed difference of opinion amongst scientific men about the truth of evolution, surpasses the fundamentalist writers of the last chapter in the art of flinging dust in the eyes of his readers. He professes to take a list of anti-evolutionist men of science from "Professor John Gerard," though he must be quite aware that *Father* John Gerard is simply a British Jesuit who has never had any connection either with science or professorship. His list covers a period of sixty years, it gives no dates, and it includes pronounced living evolutionists like Professor Driesch and Köleiker, venerable antiques like Quatrefages and Blanchard, and even advanced rationalists like Von Hartmann. His "Professor Wasmann" is another Jesuit whose clerical identity he conceals, and his "Professor Brass" is the scurrilous popular German lecturer who accused Haeckel of forgery and was disowned by his own League. In spite of this and the vindication of Haeckel's honor by forty of the most eminent scientists of Germany, McCann, in the grossest language, tells his Catholic readers—of whom, I understand, he has tens of thousands—that Haeckel was "a specialist in frauds and forgeries" and was "ignominiously exposed." I show absolutely in another Little Blue Book that this legend of "Haeckel's forgeries" is a tissue of lies which no writer can produce today without branding himself.

The book is popular in America because the author not only uses blatant language, but makes it plain that he has read a very extensive literature about the evolution of man, and it is precisely on that account that I put him in a different category from the ignorant preacher. This extensive reading he uses for the purpose of deceiving the reader. Whenever a new find of prehistoric human bones is made, there is bound to be a period of controversy, unless the type is already well known. Scores of skulls or skeletons have been discovered about which there has not been the least controversy. These McCann never mentions. He gives his readers the differences of opinion (concealing the dates) in the early stages and induces the reader to think that this is the actual state of science.

On the Java remains, for instance, scientific men have been in agreement for twenty years, but by digging up the ancient objections of Virchow and Lydekker, and concealing the dates, he conveys the impression that they are still disputed. The Piltdown remains, which he grossly describes as a few bits of bone which "a juggler could conceal in the palm of one hand"—they are the best part of a large skull and a good part of a second— he represents as still disputed, and even makes the silly suggestion that the bones were fraudulently placed in the gravel. The Mauer jaw is dismissed with the airy assurance that "Professor Wasmann" has discovered that it resembles the jaw of an Eskimo; concealing from the reader that Wasmann is a Jesuit who has no authority whatever on the subject, and that the jaw is beyond all controversy in science as an ape-like human jaw of hundreds of thousands of years ago. Even Neanderthal man, of whom we have dozens of consistent remains, is actually laughed off the stage as a disputed interpetation of a few bones! We know Neanderthal man as well as we know the true Veddahs (McCann calls them "Weedas") of Ceylon. From cover to cover the book is a synthetic cream of falsehood; and I am told that it is the most popular apologetic work of the last five years in the Roman Catholic world.

I am not in the least disposed to dismiss such a work, with all its evidence of industry, as an innocent compilation of lies told by other people, and when we rise to the higher level of what a Catholic would call the "scholars" of his Church I am equally indisposed to admit the plea of innocence. Several examples of this, such as the works of "Professor" Father Zahm and "Professor" Dr. Walsh, I have examined in other books. But the richest specimen is the *Catholic Encyclopaedia.* In the production of this work, a most expensive and richly illustrated work in sixteen large volumes, the American Catholic Church has had to employ no small share of its wealth. It professes to represent "Catholic scholarship in every part of the world," and it promises "the latest and most accurate information"— it is news to me that there are degrees of accuracy—and the use of "scientific methods." And it is a clotted mush of untruths.

One need not go far in it for illustrations of its scientific methods and most accurate information. "Adam" still has an article to himself, and he is exhibited without the least qualification as the first man. The whole of modern science is absolutely ignored, and the human race is traced to a pair of highly-endowed mortals who stole an apple and were cursed, and so their posterity degenerated from the semi-angelic level. This represents "Catholic scholarship in every part of the world."

You wonder if the dear old Deluge lingers in the affections of these Catholic scholars along with Adam and Eve, and incredible as it may seem, it does. Here, however, the cloven foot of the "scientific methods" is just perceptible. It is admitted that there are scientific reasons for supposing that the flood was not "geographically universal," and that it did not, as

Christian scholars used to say, occur between 2000 and 3000 B.C., but earlier. This lands the author in a bog of difficulties: of which he seems quite insensible. The same *Genesis* which compels the man to hold that the entire human race was destroyed except Noah and his family says explicitly that the waters went high above the top of "all the high hills" on earth (viii, 19), yet it was, the writer says, only a local flood! And not a word is said about the little difficulties concerning the animals or the notorious deluge-story of the Babylonians. The man had his tongue in his cheek.

Nearly every article exhibits the same gross perversion of scientific and historical data in the service of ancient myths, and the articles which directly deal with science are just as bad. Probably the most important controversial article in the whole *Encyclopaedia,* in view of the circumstances of our time, is that on "Evolution." Apparently the American bishops could not find in America any Catholic writer who knew sufficient science to write this article, so they had recourse to two European Jesuits: Father Wasmann, whose quaint views on evolution are an entertainment to his colleagues in natural history (he is an expert on ants), and Father Muckermann, who teaches "biology" in a Jesuit school in Holland and is an expert on nothing.

The article is delicious, though I should ascribe the greater part of the misstatements in this case to sheer ignorance of the subject. We are told that evolution is quite disproved because the earliest fossil remains we have are the remains of quite advanced animals like trilobites. It appears that this is the science taught in Jesuit colleges; that, in fact, the most illustrious of these Jesuit teachers that the Catholic organizers of the work could hire, is a man who does not know the bare rudiments of the story. Any boy of fifteen in a geology class could tell these "Catholic scholars" why there are no fossils until just before the Cambrian and why during millions of years animals left no remains. I distinctly remember that this particular "objection to evolution" was in circulation more than forty years ago. Now it is "the latest and most accurate information."

Most of the points in the article are of much the same value.

In connection with the evolution of man, however, the evidence is quite untruthfully represented, and the Catholic reader is, as usual, deceived into thinking that the theory is based upon a few disputed bones. The Ape-Man of Java is roundly stated to be an ape—there is only one man who now holds that eccentric opinion—and we are told, quite falsely, that there are twelve different theories of Neanderthal man, the best known of all prehistoric races. The gem of the article is, however, an attempt (the only one I have ever seen) to explain away the vestigial organs. It appears that they may have been useful in earlier members of the same species! Well, my Catholic friend, you may take your choice. The writer of this most important article in your most important work either does not know the A B C of his subject or he is grossly deceiving innocent readers. If you hesitate to think this, try to imagine early man—say Adam and Eve—with the vestigial organs developed and active: with pointed mobile ears, a thick coat of hair all over the body, a third eyelid, a tail, male breasts developed, guts inflated like rabbits, etc., etc. Our glorious protoparents must have been funnier birds than ever dawned upon the imagination of a humorous artist.

The truth is that these Jesuit writers, indeed most of the "Catholic scholars" of this *Encyclopaedia* who have to defend the faith against skeptics and Protestants, are both liars and innocent purveyors of lies. They rarely know the subject, if it involves science, and they copy each other like parrots; but such real difficulties as they do understand, since these are elementary and notorious, are always misrepresented and thus easily settled. One wonders once more where is the sense of humor of American Catholics. Do they really imagine that a Jesuit priest teaching what he calls biology (which probably means a smattering of six different sciences) in an obscure school in Holland can so lightly and easily dispose of the unanimous conclusions of the hunderds of scientific experts all over the world?

It confirms the thesis which I press upon my readers, that history is more hostile to religion than science is, when we notice that there is little science in this *Encyclopaedia,* but a very great deal of history; and it is even worse than the science. The writers of the historical articles do know the facts, as a rule, and their one concern is to prop up the tottering faith by suppressing inconvenient facts and using fraudulent evidence for those which seem convenient. They are, as a whole, worse than Father Muckermann and Father Zahm, and, vulgarity apart, [than] McCann. A stream of historical lies flows through the work from the first volume to the last. The historical relations of the Church to science are, of course, entirely misrepresented, and every other historical issue which I have treated is quite dishonestly presented.

In one of my books, *The Popes and Their Church,* I sketched the real history of the Church on the lines which I have followed in the historical books of this series. Then, in order to explain to the reader how it is that there can be any educated Catholics in the world if that is the genuine history of the Roman Church, I turned to the *Catholic Encyclopaedia* and described what it said about each pope and each phase of history. I thus made a portentous collection of lies. Except that some of the early saints and martyrs were sacrificed—this gave an air of critical scholarship, I suppose, but the facts are now too notorious—the facts of history were manipulated, mutilated, and falsified with an unscrupulousness that was really appalling. I would undertake to select a thousand lies from each volume of this *Catholic Encyclopaedia.*

A third kind of lie which abounds in it is the biographical. Men who notoriously quitted the Church and never returned to it are, if they are men of genius or distinction, unblushingly claimed as Roman Catholics, and others who simply permitted a final ceremony to please their families, or had the ceremony performed while they were unconscious, are mendaciously represented as sincerely reconciled. In a recent book of this series I showed this in the case of "the great Catholic scientist" Pasteur, who was not at all a Catholic. Beethoven and Mozart, both very deliberate seceders, are claimed without a qualification; though Mozart was never even formally readmitted and Beethoven expressly said that his admission of the priest in his last hours was only a matter of accommodation. The famous agnostic author Littre is included, though the writer must have known well that he was merely daubed with the Church's oils while he lay unconscious. In every case the essential details are suppressed or falsified. It is the same in the case of inconvenient men like Galileo and Vesalius and Roger Bacon—the settled facts are grossly misstated—and it is even worse in the case of heretics like Luther, Hus, the Albigensians, etc., etc. In short, the Catholic position is to such an enormous extent based upon history that there are in this symposium of the Church's best living scholars a thousand historical and biographical articles which, tested by the recognized teaching of modern history, reek with mendacity and trickery.

The fluency with which this is done is, of course, explained by the well-known Catholic rule that the faithful shall not read any book which is "against faith or morals." Outsiders naturally imagine that a Catholic is forbidden only to read books which have been put on the famous Index of Prohibited Books. Many are therefore genuinely puzzled at the apparent indifference of Catholics to the untruths which abound in their literature, since it is possible for them to consult hundreds of standard works of science or history which expose the errors. But this is an entire misunderstanding. The Index is an antiquated weapon which the pope rarely uses. Every Catholic is given to understand that it is a "mortal" or deadly sin (entailing eternal damnation) to read any books, whether on the Index or no, which are against the faith; and, naturally, any book which criticizes or corrects the Catholic untruths is against the faith. No book of mine is on the Index, yet the clergy insists that if a Catholic reads one of these skeptical Little Blue Books he incurs hell as surely, though possibly at a slightly lower temperature, as if he committed a murder or rape.

This gives security to the Catholic writer, and it at the same time enhances his guilt. This discipline and the clerical insistence on a natural birth rate are the two great secrets of the comparative success of the Church in keeping some millions of Americans in subjection to its weird dogmas. One might conclude that this makes it peculiarly difficult to approach the

Catholic believer. A man is supposed to ask permission of the priest, in the confessional, if he wants to read a critical book! But in point of fact the Catholic laity are becoming impatient of this tyranny and begin to perceive that it is a clerical stratagem. The adherent of any other creed in the world may read both sides, but the Catholic may not. He begins to wonder if truth really requires such drastic protection from criticism, and he is today reading skeptical literature. And, as I said in the case of the fundamentalist, he ought first of all to be convinced of the untruthfulness of his literature. He will resent the deception and be more disposed to give a dispassionate consideration to the evidence.

6

Modernist Morals

I have explained several times that I am far less concerned with modernists than with less liberal believers. Of the fifty million professing or churchgoing Christians of America probably thirty million are fundamentalists or Catholics: both fine bodies of men and women, pathetically miseducated in all that pertains to religion, and offering a splendid field for a judicious and vigorous campaign of enlightenment. The unveracity of their literature and preaching, which actually is their most effective bond of union, is their most vulnerable and accessible feature. I have ceased to write large academic works and have for years urged rationalists to concentrate on the publication of cheap and effective works for the enlightenment of these millions.

Of the remaining twenty million churchgoers at least fifteen million are, according to their sects, in much the same position as the fundamentalists and Catholics. Their faith is in most respects based upon the same foundation of historical untruths. They may not oppose evolution, though they never clearly confront its implications as regards God and the spirituality of the soul. They may not insist on a literal acceptance of *Genesis,* but of the sources of its legends and the circumstances in which the Old Testament was composed, as we now have it, they know no more than the fundamentalist or the Catholic. They cling to the blood-atonement, the virgin birth, the resurrection, the miracles, the unique morality of Christ, and the preternatural triumph and entire beneficence in history of the Christian religion. Hence they ground their faith on the same mass of historical untruths and their literature is open to the same criticisms.

There remain a few million who may be gathered together in the category called modernists: in which I would put not only those who modernize the more elaborate creeds of the Episcopal or Methodist Churches, but the more liberal Congregationalists and Theistic Unitarians. They are very apt to plead, somewhat petulantly, that, since they have purged the creed of its medieval errors, the critic of Christianity ought to address himself chiefly, or even exclusively, to them. And the reply is that they are not of sufficient practical importance. Not only are they a small minority, and if skeptical education is wisely conducted they will remain a minority, but they are not particularly mischievous. These are not the fanatics who would tyrannize over their neighbors and use the arm of the law to put the yoke of their own code on the necks of those who do not accept it. They may support, but do not initiate, prohibitions and inhibitions and sexhibitions. Most of us are interested in religion, not as an academic question of Truth, but because of its mischievous interferences with social life and the liberty of the individual.

To say, however, that we neglect "intellectual Christianity" and attack only the feebler victim is ludicrously untrue. The belief in the existence of God is as vulnerable as the belief in the miracles of Christ, and a skeptic is just as willing to attack one as the other. The belief in the immortality of the soul is really easier to refute than the belief in the Trinity or the Immaculate Conception, and the modernist can hardly complain of any lack of criticism of his arguments—which have nothing modern about them—for that belief. The notion of any modernists, that in sacrificing the Old Testament, the Trinity, the Atonement, and so on, they have retired to firmer ground and can now set aside all anxiety about the teaching of science or history, is merely amusing. A dozen Little Blue Books of this series are directed against them as well as against the old types of believers, and my task was not in the least more difficult with these books.

With the characteristically modernist game of modernizing the phraseology of the old creeds, or putting modern meanings into old formulae, I decline to waste my time. It is merely their domestic concern if they find themselves under an ecclesiastical discipline which compels them to repeat the old formulae. Most of us prefer the freedom of the open road. We are more disposed to tell the bishops to put their aprons and croziers in the Metropolitan Museum and not try to be funny. The whole business is exasperating. The modernist does not find a new meaning in the Trinity, the Atonement, inspiration, revelation, etc. The words have only one meaning. They were chosen by clerical authorities in the Dark Ages just because they expressed that meaning and not the views of our modernists: which were quite well known as the views of heretics in the early Church. The game does not interest me, but, as I said, I recognize that it is a painful domestic necessity.

Apart from all this verbiage the modernist position, the new religious position which is held to be critically impregnable, is pretty much the same as the old type of Unitarianism. It is not very much different from the religion of Voltaire and Paine. They say with Browning (one of their favorite poets), "Soul and God stand sure"; and, when we have set aside a lot of verbiage which tries to express the idea that Christ was divine but not God, they hold the "sublime and unique morality" theory and claim that Christ's personality and teaching have advanced civilization. Naturally, there is no such thing as one modernist creed. There are fifty. These people who have "rescued religion from the arena of controversy" fight each other interminably about the nature of God and immortality, the person of Christ, the extent to which we can recognize his words in the Gospels, and so on. I have got to simplify matters by saying that modernism, or the simplest expression of the Christian religion, is a belief in God, the soul, Christ as master-moralist, and Christianity as a uniquely beneficent religious institution.

And these beliefs are based upon untruths just as surely as are the beliefs of the fundamentalist, and large numbers of modernist writers are quite dishonest in repeating the untruths. They surely know that the philosophical arguments which most of them use in proving the existence and nature of God have been discarded from philosophy long ago; and that the prolonging of the story of life over hundreds of millions of years of stark brutality is, not "a greater revelation than ever of God's power," as they habitually say, but a ghastly inconsistency with belief in theism. They must know that the long and gradual evolution of man from an apelike form of twenty million years ago has put the belief in a spiritual soul in an extremely precarious position, yet they either ignore altogether this plain and important message of science or, as I have quoted one of them in a previous chapter, actually say that it has "opened great spaces for the belief in immortality." There is hardly a single writer of the school who, while he is assuring his readers that evolution is consistent with these beliefs, or even says that it has strengthened them, candidly faces the really relevant features of the story of evolution. The professors of science who belong to this school are as bad—as lacking in candor and courage and straightforwardness—as the preachers. I have given ample evidence on these points in Little Blue Books Nos. 1059, 1060, 1211, 1224, and 1229. You can lie by suppressing facts if you give your readers a general assurance that you are facing all the relevant facts.

Other Little Blue Books of this series (Nos. 1008, 1061, 1077, etc.) deal with modernist misrepresentations in other respects. They are just as false to science in their account of the nature of moral law as they are false to history when they decry pre-Christian religions and civilizations in order to give a fictitious superiority to Christianity. Indeed, here they are, if anything, rather worse than fundamentalists. It is an essential part of modernism—or the reconciliation of modern culture with Christian belief—that the work of the great biblical experts, insofar as they are fairly agreed, should be recognized. This work, however, makes it impossible for us to be confident that any act or word ascribed to Jesus in the gospels is authentic, yet the modernist goes even beyond the fundamentalist in emphasizing the unique loftiness of Christ's character and teaching. He is feverishly anxious to cover up his denial of the divinity of Christ. And the extreme modernist who says that he is indifferent to the question whether the gospels are historical or no, that it is the Christ-ideal which inspires, is not a whit better. I have shown in several books that these people never patiently analyze the character of Jesus in the gospels and never compare his "incomparable" teaching with that of the other moralists to whom, they invariably say, he is far superior. To call themselves Christians they are forced to find something unique in Christ; and it is one of the most fraudulent of all myths.

They, then, although they feel more free to recognize the blunders and crudities of the hierarchy in earlier ages, falsify the record of Christianity almost as much as their less advanced colleagues do. All modernist writers repeat the gross historical untruths which I have exposed in a dozen of these Little Blue Books: that the triumph of Christianity was moral and spiritual (see No. 1110), that the great art of the Middle Ages was inspired by religion (see No. 1136), that Christianity uplifted woman (1122), emancipated the slave (1127), and gave the world schools (1128), and so on. There is hardly a traditional untruth in regard to the services of Christianity which they do not repeat and sustain. They have no conception of the real civilizing forces in the history of Europe (the internal economic development, the Arab influence, etc.), they repeat the stale libels of the French Revolution, and they are as fluent as any in vituperating the writer who points out that seven Presidents of the United States were skeptics (No. 1203) or that modern philanthropy has its roots, not in religion, but in a Deistic-agnostic humanitarianism.

I should say that one-third of my Little Blue Books hit the modernist as hard as they hit the fundamentalist; and they hit the modernist scholar and scientist as hard as the preacher. The moment the man leaves his proper subject he repeats the conventional untruths like any other apologist. Lodge, Osborn, and Millikan are no more reliable than fashionable preachers in New York or Washington. There is something miasmic about religion. Its defense is saturated with untruth: its defenders are less critical and scrupulous in their statements than the writers in almost any other department of literature. Claims which have been annihilated hundreds of times appear weekly in the religious press and are mellifluously broadcast from a thousand pulpits. And the crowning irony is to have these people assure us that, if the modern race discards their services and abandons their creeds, it is likely to lose the quick sense of honor and truthfulness which fifteen centuries of Christian education have implanted in it.